Learning and Studying

A Research Perspective

- James Hartley

ROUTLEDGE

LONDON AND NEW YORK

First published 1998
by Routledge
11 New Fetter Lane
London EC4P 4EE

Simultaneously published in
the USA and Canada
by Routledge
29 West 35th Street, New York
NY 10001

© 1998 James Hartley

Typeset in Sabon and Futura by
Florencetype Ltd, Stoodleigh, Devon

Printed and bound in Great Britain by
Clays Ltd, St Ives PLC

*British Library Cataloguing in
Publication Data*
A catalogue record for this book is
available from the British Library

*Library of Congress Cataloging in
Publication Data*
A catalog record for this book has
been requested

ISBN 0–415–16851–1 (hbk)

ISBN 0–415–16852–X (pbk)

Contents

CONTENTS

Figures and boxes

Figures

Boxes

Tables

Series preface

The Psychology Focus series provides short, up-to-date accounts of key areas in psychology without assuming the reader's prior knowledge in the subject. Psychology is often a favoured subject area for study, since it is relevant to a wide range of disciplines such as Sociology, Education, Nursing and Business Studies. These relatively inexpensive but focused short texts combine sufficient detail for psychology specialists with sufficient clarity for non-specialists.

The series authors are academics experienced in undergraduate teaching as well as research. Each takes a key topic within their area of psychological expertise and presents a short review, highlighting important themes and including both theory and research findings. Each aspect of the topic is clearly explained with supporting glossaries to elucidate technical terms.

The series has been conceived within the context of the increasing modularisation which has been developed in higher education over the last decade

and fulfils the consequent need for clear, focused, topic-based course material. Instead of following one course of study, students on a modularisation programme are often able to choose modules from a wide range of disciplines to complement the modules they are required to study for a specific degree. It can no longer be assumed that students studying a particular module will necessarily have the same background knowledge (or lack of it!) in that subject. But they will need to familiarise themselves with a particular topic rapidly since a single module in a single topic may be only 15 weeks long, with assessments arising during that period. They may have to combine eight or more modules in a single year to obtain a degree at the end of their programme of study.

One possible problem with studying a range of separate modules is that the relevance of a particular topic or the relationship between topics may not always be apparent. In the Psychology Focus series authors have drawn where possible on practical and applied examples to support the points being made so that readers can see the wider relevance of the topic under study. Also, the study of psychology is usually broken up into separate areas, such as social psychology, developmental psychology and cognitive psychology, to take three examples. Whilst the books in the Psychology Focus series will provide excellent coverage of certain key topics within these 'traditional' areas, the authors have not been constrained in their examples and explanations and may draw on material across the whole field of psychology to help explain the topic under study more fully.

Each text in the series provides the reader with a range of important material on a specific topic. They are suitably comprehensive and give a clear account of the important issues involved. The authors analyse and interpret the material as well as present an up-to-date and detailed review of key work. Recent references are provided along with suggested further reading to allow readers to investigate the topic in more depth. It is hoped, therefore, that after following the informative review of a key topic in a Psychology Focus text, readers will not only have a clear understanding of the issues in question but will be intrigued and challenged to investigate the topic further.

Chapter 1

How psychologists study learning and studying

T HIS CHAPTER CONSIDERS the advantages and disadvantages of different methods used in psychological research in the field of learning and studying. Particular attention is paid to what readers should consider when studying research articles. The chapter concludes with a summary of the arguments made in each of the following chapters.

■

This text has been written for the Psychology Focus series. This means that it is mostly orientated towards psychology and towards psychology students. Many of the examples in the text are drawn from studying psychology, and much of the advice given is derived from this work. However, a great deal of the content can be applied to other disciplines, and this means that everyone should find it valuable.

Learning and Studying: A Research Perspective is not a traditional text about study skills. It is a text about how psychologists study learning and studying, what they have achieved, and what they can achieve in this area. Thus any advice that is given about learning and study skills – and there will be plenty – is incidental to this aim.

The nature of psychological investigation

Psychologists are concerned with assessing the evidence for a particular point of view. In the field of learning and studying there is a great deal of opinion – much of it contradictory. Compare, for example, 'You can't teach an old dog new tricks' with 'You are never too old to learn'. The job of psychologists is to try and determine which opinion is right. Needless to say, they immediately begin to qualify any bald statements such as the two just given. They seek to sort out to whom such statements apply, under which conditions, and so on. They seek to take measurements – of different kinds and **validity** – and argue amongst themselves about what it is appropriate to do, how it can be done, and how the results can be interpreted.

Curiously enough, researchers often try to seek evidence for answers to questions that have already been ignored. Thus they end up trying to change and modify the effects of previous decisions. In the early 1990s, for instance, most universities in the UK modularised their courses without any evidence concerning what the advantages and disadvantages of this might be. Psychologists are now involved in assessing the effects of that decision.

Methods in psychological research

Table 1.1 shows, in a summary form, the different kinds of methods that psychologists use, together with their strengths and limitations. One implication here – if each method has advantages and disadvantages – is that psychologists should employ as many methods as they can in combination. However, what appears to have happened historically is that **quantitative** methods have been preferred to **qualitative** methods, and this is certainly true in the field of learning and studying. More recently, however, there has been a greater interest in using qualitative methods in this field, and some studies now use both approaches. Robson (1993) provides a useful text that clarifies the strengths and weaknesses of the full range of methodologies open to researchers in this field.

Psychologists generally use the different methods shown in Table 1.1 to tackle different types of questions. In the field of

TABLE 1.1 Typical research methods used in psychology, together with their advantages and disadvantages

Method:	Experiments	Tests, questionnaires and surveys
Description of method	Controlled investigations that study cause-and-effect relationships through the random allocation of participants to control or treatment conditions	Way of obtaining information regarding behaviour, beliefs and abilities at a particular time and place
Form of data obtained	Quantitative ('hard data'; statistical, verifiable by replication)	Quantitative/qualitative ('soft data'; descriptive, practical)
Advantages of method	1. Control of independent variables 2. Permits causal inferences 3. Large numbers allow results to be generalised	1. Easily administered 2. Easily scored and analysed 3. Possibly large and representative samples
Disadvantages of method	1. The ability to generalise to real-world situations is limited 2. Little attention to individual participants 3. Possibly raises ethical issues	1. Participants rarely allocated at random to conditions, so little concern with cause and effect 2. May not be able to generalise beyond a specific time, place and test content 3. Possible discrepancies between real-life behaviour and test behaviour 4. Often low return rates

TABLE 1.1 Continued

Method:	Naturalistic observations	Interviews and case studies
Description of method	Observations of real-life situations, as in classrooms, work settings or halls of residence	Intensive studies of single individuals, which draw general conclusions about experience and behaviour
Form of data obtained	Qualitative	Qualitative
Advantages of method	1. Wide applicability of results 2. Understanding of behaviour in natural contexts	Highly detailed information, including the historical context
Disadvantages of method	1. Loss of experimental control 2. Possibility that the presence of the observer may influence the observed behaviour	1. Ability to generalise from the information drastically curtailed by the small sample sizes 2. Lack of reliable data

Source: Adapted from *In Search of the Human Mind* by Robert J. Sternberg, copyright © 1995, Harcourt Brace International, reproduced with the permission of the author and publishers.

learning and studying, for example, we typically find **experimental methods** used to address issues such as whether or not one method of notetaking is preferable to another; **survey methods** to assess why certain people drop out from higher education; and interviews and **case histories** to uncover how different types of learners take different approaches to, say, essay writing. However, as indicated above, these different methods are now beginning to be used in combination. Thus, for example, in studies of mature students, 'archival' methods (where one examines college examination records over time) are now being supplemented by illustrative case histories and interview studies (see Chapter 4).

One particular quantitative statistical technique that has developed since the 1970s, and one that has been used a great deal in the field of learning and studying, is that of **meta-analysis**. The aim of this technique is to allow researchers both to summarise the results from many studies on the same issue, and to compare sub-groups of studies within this overall sample. This is done by calculating a summary statistic – called an average 'effect-size' – that indicates the general conclusion that can be reached when the results from several studies on the same issue are pooled together. Thus, for example, as we shall see in Chapter 6, Kulik *et al.* (1980) pooled together the individual effect-sizes from fifty-nine separate studies of computer-based learning versus traditional instruction at college level and arrived at an average effect-size of 0.25.

Such effect-sizes are normally measured in **standard deviations** – so an overall effect-size of 0.25 means that the computer groups (overall) gained a quarter of a standard deviation above the **mean** score and standard deviation obtained by the traditional groups. Cohen (1987) suggests that effect-sizes can be interpreted as follows:

0.0   no effect – the groups are identical
0.2   small effect
0.5   medium effect
0.8   large effect.

So the effect-size of 0.25 found by Kulik *et al.* in 1980 suggested that computer-aided learning (at that time) had only a small advantage over traditional methods of learning.

The advantage of this meta-analytic technique is that all the known studies can be included – including the ones that failed to find an effect, or found them in the reverse direction to the general trend. The disadvantages emerge when one considers how the authors of these meta-analytic studies decide which studies to include, and which to leave out, and which variables to pool together. Some investigators of individual studies do not always report all the data necessary for such studies to be included in the ensuing meta-analysis. Furthermore, the results of some studies – particularly those that find no significant differences – may not have been published. Other studies may be fatally flawed, even though they provide the necessary statistics for a meta-analysis, and so on.

The most common criticism of meta-analytic studies is that 'Garbage in leads to garbage out'! Clearly then, when reading a meta-analytic study, readers need to read with caution. I would hope that, after reading Chapter 3 for example, readers might take a critical view of some aspects of the meta-analytic study published by Chen and Rada (1996). Here, these investigators pooled the results from separate studies on the effects of spatial ability, **locus of control, field dependency** and **learning style** on students' use of **hypertext** (see Chapter 6) under the general heading of 'active' **cognitive styles** and compared them with the results from other studies of 'less-active' ones. I imagine that, after reading Chapter 3, readers might think it odd to combine such studies together.

Reading research critically

Of course, we should read everything critically, not just meta-analyses. So my strictures above also apply to reading the articles that I cite in this text.

Indeed, it is always worth following up relevant citations if you can. By doing so you can gain a fuller picture of the issues involved. Often in this text I have had to summarise the main findings of, say, a twenty-page report in a few sentences. Such a summary may well miss out important considerations. It is actually very interesting to compare actual original (primary) accounts with secondary (textbook) versions of them. Often the over-simple conclusions drawn by secondary authors have to be taken with a pinch of salt.

In the following paragraphs I suggest some things to look out for when reading research articles in psychology (see also Girden, 1996). The best articles contain none of these faults, but some might contain one or two. Hopefully, none will contain them all!

Table 1.2 shows that journal articles typically have a set series of sections and a standard set of conventions, which allows for ease of communication. Much academic learning is about understanding research reports in journals and that is why it is important to appreciate what each section is trying to achieve.

Some problems that may occur in these sections are as follows:

TABLE 1.2 The standard sections of a journal article

Abstract

Introduction

Method

Results

Discussion

Conclusions

References

1 The abstract Abstracts contain statements about the background and aims of the study, the participants and the main results and conclusions. Since such abstracts can be published and read independently of the article (e.g., in electronic databases) it is important that there are no misleading statements or overgeneralisations. Sometimes all the caveats of the discussion disappear and a rather oversimplified conclusion emerges. This conclusion then gets cited elsewhere by people who have only read the abstract. (So don't rely on abstracts alone when doing your own literature reviews!)

2 The introduction Introductions generally fall into parts (Swales and Feak, 1994). First, the background to the study is given. Then the author makes a 'move', i.e. critiquing ('However, there has been no research on . . .') or linking separate areas of research ('In this study I shall see if the differences in the findings from these two sets of studies can be resolved by . . .'). Making this move then leads to the hypothesis to be tested.

Introductions can be problematical for several reasons.

- The author may cite too many references – suggesting a scholarship that is false, since it does not help the reader to discriminate between the key papers.
- The author may set up a one-sided argument, or a 'straw man', by citing only part of the literature available.

- The author may erroneously dismiss or be unaware of previous research, or just be inaccurate (e.g., there are enormous generalisations made about research findings on notetaking that Chapter 5 shows to be fallacious.)

3 The method The method chosen has to be appropriate to the task in hand (see Table 1.1) and so too do the statistical procedures used. Issues to consider here are the precision with which the method is given (can it be repeated from this description?), whether or not it is ethical (are some learners deprived of a learning experience that they might have benefited from?), and how the participants were chosen (are they just students who happened to be at hand?). It is important that the samples be representative, whatever their size (e.g., it is hard to accept the following conclusions, however much we may agree with them, that 'an increasing number of students have no choice but to do paid work during their courses to be able to continue their studies and meet basic living costs . . . and that the need to work and study is putting them under increasing pressure and the quality of their results is being affected' [National Union of Students, 1996] when we are told that the response rate to the questionnaire on which these conclusions were based was 7.3%).

In comparison studies we need to look for how participants are assigned to groups. For example, is this done (1) at random, (2) by comparing different classes in the same year, or (3) by giving the new technique to this year's class, and comparing the results with last year's? Note that each method has its difficulties. Different classes may not be the same – they may have different tutors with different degrees of involvement in the study, and so on. Classes from different years may differ on many measures – so there is a need for both before and after measures for both groups. (Many studies, for example those described in Chapter 4, are flawed because we don't know if the two groups being compared differed or not at the *outset* of the study.)

Finally, we need to consider when the measurements are made. Often tests are given at the end of a comparison study to measure, for example, immediate recall. But it might also be important to know if the effects persist over time, or whether or not some methods produce results that are less liable to decay than others. Multiple-choice tests given, for example, at the end of a module may encourage students to memorise by rote for that module and then promptly forget what they have learned.

4 The results   The results sections – of quantitative studies – are often difficult to read. Some problems arise here from poorly presented tables and graphs, as well as misleading ones. So it is a good idea to look at these data *before* reading what the authors have to say about them. Sometimes you will be surprised – what seem to be small differences may well be described as **statistically significant** and treated as though they were practically important when, for example, the difference might only be 2 or 3% on an examination.

Furthermore, different readers might have different concerns from those of the authors of papers. Thus, for example, when Gibbs *et al*. (1996) report that there is a decrease in examination scores as module sizes increase, we need to note that the average decrease is from 57% (for modules with 10–20 students) to 55% (for modules with over 70 students). Administrators might not be too upset with these figures – unlike students and academics.

We also need to look carefully at the intervals used on the vertical and horizontal scales of graphs. In the case just cited, the intervals on the vertical scale used by Gibbs *et al*. run from 54.4% to 57.4% rather than from, say, 0% to 100%, and thus their graph massively exaggerates their findings. Similar distortions occur with tabular presentations. Table 1.3 shows, for example, the results of an experiment conducted by Rosenthal and Jacobson (1968). Here the data show the number of children who gained 10, 20 or 30 IQ points in an experiment where the teacher was led to believe that such pupils were likely to show an academic 'spurt'. The point to note here is that in this table each group *also contains members of the group below it*. Rosenthal and Jacobson presumably feel that if pupils gain 20 or 30 IQ points it is reasonable to include them within the group that gains at least 10 points. . .

TABLE 1.3 Percentage of pupils gaining at least 10, 20 or 30 total IQ points

IQ gain at least	Control group (N = 95)	Experimental group (N = 19)
10 points*	49	79
20 points**	19	47
30 points	5	21

Notes:
* Includes children gaining 20 and 30 points or more.
**Includes children gaining 30 points or more.
Source: From *Pygmalion in the Classroom* by R. Rosenthal and L. Jacobson, copyright © 1968 by Holt Rinehart and Winston, reprinted by permission of the authors and the publisher.

Effects can be exaggerated in other ways too. One particular thing to look out for in studies of learning and studying is the use of (selected) quotations or data from individuals, rather than from the group, to make a point more effectively.

Also, in reading the results sections we need to check the appropriateness of the statistics used. In some studies, for instance, means are sometimes accompanied by standard deviations that are considerably larger than the actual means themselves. What does this imply about the data, and what methods of presentation of **central tendency** should have been used?

To take another example, sometimes the mean scores on different questionnaire items are ranked in order of decreasing size, but if we look carefully we might find that the means are actually very similar. In one study, for example, means of 5.07, 5.06, 5.05 and 5.04 were ranked 7, 8, 9 and 10 respectively, and this implied a much greater difference between them than in fact there was. What was worse, however, was that a mean of 5.41 on one item was ranked 1 but a mean of 5.41 on another item was ranked 2. (When I queried this with the authors, they replied that the means had been rounded to two decimal places and that in fact the mean of rank 1 was higher than that of rank 2 when this third decimal place was taken into account!) Such spurious accuracy seems to me to be inappropriate, especially if further calculations are done on the ranked data.

11

Finally, we need to look for data that, for some reason, are not included. In one study of the performance of **Access** students at university (that is, students who come to university by a non-traditional route – see Chapter 5), for example, the author calmly stated that degree results were crude measures, and thus *she did not report them*, preferring instead to concentrate on the experiences of individual students. So, we need to look for problems like this and, for example, for data on sex differences, order effects and possible interactions between the main variables that might have been omitted.

5 The discussion and the conclusions The things to look out for in the discussion and the conclusions, assuming that there are no problems with the previous sections, are similar to those in the introduction and the abstract. Here we need to check whether or not the limitations to the study (and there are bound to be some) are appropriately acknowledged and discussed, or played down, or simply ignored. Similarly, we also need to decide whether or not the main findings are appropriately considered, and not exaggerated. So some questions to ask here might be how well the results are interpreted in relation to the original hypotheses, and what suggestions are made about how best to continue this research in the future.

In this section I have tried to suggest that we need to read research reports critically. In my view, this is perhaps the main study skill that students should practise.

An overview of *Learning and Studying: A Research Perspective*

I have been highly conscious when writing the above that I have been offering a counsel of perfection. Undoubtedly, in the ensuing pages the observant reader will notice that I too have failed to be as perfect as I should be. I, too, on occasions have used quotations, selected examples and made statements not supported by evidence. And the reason for this, shared with other authors of scientific papers, is that I have been trying to weave an argument.

The reader's job is to assess the value of this argument and the evidence used to support it. If you think the argument weak, you will need to seek contrary evidence, or at least consider how such evidence might be obtained.

What does this argument look like? In Chapter 2, I suggest that there are different ways of thinking about learning, and these have different implications for instruction. In Chapter 3, I examine how there can be no one way of learning – individuals differ in a variety of ways, and so do institutions and their courses. In Chapter 4, I consider in more detail research on the performance of mature students at university. Here I argue that such students are not so very different from traditional-entry ones, and that all students, regardless of their age and experience, can be taught to be better learners. In Chapter 5, I consider attempts to do this – both historically and today; and in Chapter 6, I examine learning with new technology as an example of new possibilities in this respect. Finally, in Chapter 7, I discuss limitations of the current methods of assessment, and how newer methods can help students to achieve **life-long learning** skills.

Throughout the text I also make passing remarks (without citing any specific evidence) about how the current situation in higher education – declining resources, increasing numbers, modularisation, etc. – all militate against effective learning and studying. As I put down my pen (well, switch off my word-processor) I suggest that it is up to you – the readers – to fight against this.

Further reading

Girden, E. R. (1996) *Evaluating Research Articles from Start to Finish*, London: Sage. This text uses examples of good and flawed studies to show the reader how to gauge the quality of both quantitative and qualitative studies in the social sciences.

Robson, C. (1993) *Real World Research: A Resource for Social Scientists and Practitioner-Researchers*, Oxford: Blackwell. Few statistical texts are riveting, but this one is more interesting than most. As the title implies, Robson considers the pros and cons of different methods of doing research in 'messy' real-life situations.

Learning theory in practice

THIS CHAPTER IS divided into two main sections. In the first part I outline principles of learning from behavioural, cognitive and phenomenological psychology that may be useful for instruction. In the second part I illustrate some of these principles in practice.

■

The relationship between theory and practice is a symbiotic one: theory contributes to practice, and practice contributes to theory. In the last two decades, in the area of instruction, this has been very clear. There has been a swing against the theories that guided the earlier practice and present practice has influenced the latest theories.

In particular, there has been a marked rise and fall in the use of Skinner's **operant conditioning** approach to the design of instruction and instructional materials. Practice has shown us how human learning is much more complex than this approach suggests. The notion that human learners are passive recipients of instruction who can be **reinforced** in a variety of ways has been replaced by the view that learners are active processors of information using a variety of strategies to remember and utilise knowledge (strategies which they can switch on and off in different contexts), and that learners are very flexible.

In considering these ideas, however, we must recognise that operant conditioning and reinforcement still play an important part in human learning. Behaviour is almost always affected by its consequences, and it would be foolish to cast out this baby with the bathwater. Reinforcement is one technique amongst many that can be used to let learners know how well they are succeeding – a cardinal principle in successful learning.

Psychologists follow many different philosophies and, as we move through time, fashions come and go. In the first part of this chapter I shall describe principles of learning derived from three different philosophical positions. In the second part I shall provide illustrations of these principles in practice. What, then, are these principles? They are:

- principles emphasised in stimulus-response (**behavioural**) psychology;
- principles emphasised in **cognitive** psychology;
- principles emphasised in social and **phenomenological** psychology.

As we shall see, some of these principles overlap, but most have a distinctive flavour.

Principles emphasised in behavioural psychology

Behavioural psychology focuses upon the effects of the consequences of doing something on the subsequent repetition of that behaviour. Thus reinforced activities increase, and non-reinforced ones decline. As far as learning is concerned then the emphasis is laid upon external events and the acquisition of responses and habits. So the following are key principles of learning in this context:

Activity is important Learning is better when the learner is active rather than passive. As Hilgard and Bower (1975) put it, '"Learning by doing" is still an acceptable slogan'. This does not mean that people do not learn anything if they remain passive, but that they are likely to learn more if they are actively involved in the learning.

Repetition, generalisation, discrimination are key notions If learning is to become appropriate to a wide (or narrow) range of stimuli, then these notions imply that frequent practice – and

17

practice in varied contexts – is necessary for learning to take place. And, as·we know, skills – of any kind – are not acquired without considerable practice (e.g., see Ericsson and Charness, 1994).

Reinforcement is the cardinal motivator The effects of the consequences on subsequent behaviour are important – whether they be extrinsic (reward from a teacher) or intrinsic (self-reward). As Hilgard and Bower (1975) described it, 'While there are some lingering questions over details, it is generally found that positive reinforcers (rewards, successes) are to be preferred to negative events (punishments, failures)'.

Learning is helped when the objectives are clear Teachers who espouse a behavioural philosophy emphasise the need for 'behavioural objectives'. Behavioural objectives state what it is that the learner will be expected to be able to do at the end of the learning session. These expectations are usually expressed in terms of behaviours that can be measured, such as, 'At the end of the programme respondents will be able to calculate three measures of central tendency (mean, median and mode) with 95% accuracy.' To achieve these objectives, tasks are often broken down into carefully sequenced stages following a task-analysis.

Principles emphasised in cognitive psychology

Compared with behavioural psychology, cognitive psychology focuses on internal events. Learning results from inferences, expectations and making connections. Instead of acquiring habits, learners acquire plans and strategies, and prior knowledge is important. So the following are key principles of learning in this context:

Instruction should be well organised The hallmark of good instruction is that it is clearly organised (although one person's organisation may be different from another's). Well-organised material is easier to learn and to remember than is badly organised material.

Similarly, instruction should be clearly structured Subject matters are said to have inherent structures – logical relationships between key ideas and concepts – which link the parts together. Well-structured materials are easier to learn and to remember.

The perceptual features of the task are important Learners attend selectively to different features of the environment, so the way in which a problem is displayed to learners is important in helping them to understand it. (Giving learners an outline in advance that conveys the structure of the topic to be covered provides an appropriate illustration.)

Prior knowledge is important For people to acquire something new it must fit in with what they already know. The job of the tutor is to show how the new material fits in with what has gone before, and to indicate in which ways it is new or different. Work on **'advance-organisers'** is relevant here (e.g., see Griffin and Tulbert, 1995).

Differences between individuals are important in how they affect learning As well as differences in intellectual ability and personality, differences in 'cognitive style' or methods of approach also affect learning (see Chapter 3).

Cognitive feedback gives information to learners about their success or failure concerning the task in hand This feedback may be intrinsic or extrinsic. In stimulus–response (S–R) theory the term 'reinforcement' is often used in this sense of 'providing information' rather than simply as a 'reward'. Another term commonly used here is 'knowledge of results'.

Finally, *learning with understanding* is better than learning by **rote**, or learning without understanding.

Principles emphasised in social and phenomenological psychology

Phenomenological psychology focuses on feelings, emotions and experience. Knowledge is gained by living, and experience is

19

defined by 'what is in the head' rather than 'what is out there'. So the following are key principles of learning in this context:

Learning is a natural process   Human beings have a natural propensity for learning – we cannot stop doing it. People are by nature curious beings who constantly absorb information: we are natural decision-makers and problem-solvers. Learning is not something that we do at school and nowhere else.

Social situations affect learning   Learning is rarely an isolated event. The group atmosphere of learning (competition vs. co-operation, authoritarianism vs. democracy, and different value systems held by tutors and learners) will affect both success and satisfaction in learning.

The purposes and goals of learning are important   Learners have needs, goals and purposes, which provide important motivators for learning and for the setting of future goals. Many decisions about what to learn result from long-term goals which may have been decided on much earlier. (The importance of such goals is, of course, also relevant to cognitive theories.)

Choice, relevance and responsibility are important factors in learning   Learning is better when the material to be learned is personally relevant, and when the learners are responsible for their own learning. Significant learning, it is argued, only takes place when learners choose what they want to learn, how they want to learn it, and when they want to learn it (Holt, 1982a).

Learning best takes place in a realistic setting   Learning is best achieved in real-life contexts rather than in abstract and decontextualised situations (like lecture theatres and classrooms). Similarly, assessment is best carried out in real-life contexts rather than in decontextualised ones.

Meaning is a personal thing   Many people consider knowledge to be external, objective and static. Others, however, consider knowledge to be internal, subjective and fluid. People – individuals and groups – are the sources of knowledge, and thus knowledge is socially constructed (see Duffy and Jonassen, 1992, and Chapter 5).

Discussion about learning is important Discussion between students and teachers can emphasise meaningful explanations and sense-making activities – which is quite the opposite of rote learning. Knowledge creation is a shared rather than an individual process. Learners interpret and elaborate on incoming information, especially when discussing it with others.

Self-regulation – monitoring one's learning – is an important skill As learners progress, they assume more and more responsibility for monitoring their own learning. As they get older learners select or develop their own learning strategies, goals and objectives (Schunk and Zimmerman, 1994).

Learners' conceptions of learning change Learning involves conceptual changes in students, not just the accretion of new knowledge. As learners develop they move from an objectivist concept of what learning is about (e.g., facts) to a **constructivistic** one (e.g., everything is relative). (This will be discussed further in Chapter 5.)

Anxiety and emotion affect learning Learning is not just a cognitive process. Learning that involves the emotions and feelings as well as the intellect is often the most lasting and most pervasive kind.

These different approaches to learning overlap, despite the almost antagonistic philosophies being espoused as we move across the spectrum from behavioural to phenomenological accounts. Most teachers and learners will recognise most of the principles of learning that I have described, and most will utilise them as they think appropriate.

Different researchers have tried to encapsulate different sets of approaches under the heading of teaching styles, but the number of proposed styles has varied. Bennett (1976), for instance, described twelve primary-school teaching styles, before collapsing these to three. Pratt (1992) discussed five **conceptions of teaching**. In a university context Ramsden (1992) described three main teaching styles as shown in Table 2.1.

TABLE 2.1 Three main teaching styles

Teaching can be conceived of as:

●   Telling, or transmitting information – a behavioural approach.
●   Organising students' activities – a cognitive approach.
●   Making learning possible – a phenomenological approach.

Source: After Ramsden, 1992.

In terms of this chapter the three styles described in Table 2.1 seem to correspond to the behavioural, cognitive and phenomenological approaches discussed above. The first style emphasises that students must remember facts and information. The second style suggests that if the students are active in an organised way they will learn something worthwhile (which again may be facts and information). The third style is consistent with the idea that learning is something personal to the learner and, in a formal classroom setting, arises from an interaction between the tutor, the student and the subject.

In this chapter I now want to illustrate examples of these approaches in practice but, before I do so, I reiterate that most people subscribe to principles in all three categories as appropriate.

Applications in the behavioural tradition

There are today several examples of teaching methods which demonstrate an application of the traditional S–R approach. Work along these lines can be found in situations involving animal training (e.g., with dogs for the blind, or for customs officers); in special schools for the physically and learning disabled; and in self-improvement training for people with inadequate social skills.

The example I would like to describe most fully in this section is that known as the **'Keller Plan'** (after its creator, Fred

Keller) or **PSI** (personalised system of instruction), or just simply as **'behavioural instruction'** (Keller, 1968). The main feature of this kind of instruction – which has been widely used in introductory courses at the tertiary level of education – is that students work on their own at their own pace reading units (or chapters) of text. Each student then has to demonstrate mastery of the unit (usually by successfully taking a multiple-choice and/or short-answer factual-recall test) before he or she is allowed to proceed to the next unit. Typically students are expected to score 90% or more on each test. If they fail to reach this criterion they can re-study or receive remedial instruction before they try again. Most of the organisation and repeated testing is carried out by other more senior students or 'proctors'. Lectures are occasionally given as a source of motivation rather than instruction.

Many different procedures are possible within this general framework (e.g., the mastery of the units may be paced, contracts may be established for various amounts of work done, and so on) but, in general terms, behavioural instruction combines behavioural with social learning: the students do the work when they want to do it, they learn with peers, they achieve self-paced mastery performance and immediate knowledge of results.

Assessments of behavioural instruction and of variants on it by (Kulik *et al.*, 1979) have shown it to be remarkably effective. Kulik *et al.* carried out a meta-analysis using data from seventy-five comparison studies of PSI and conventional instruction. They found that PSI was superior in forty-eight out of sixty-one studies that were evaluated using class tests, and in fifty-seven out of sixty-one studies that reported final examination scores. Kulik *et al.* concluded (an earlier review) by saying, 'In our judgement, this is the most impressive record achieved by a teaching method in higher education. It stands in stark contrast to the inconclusive results of earlier comparisons of college teaching methods.'

Today there are still PSI courses in operation (e.g., see Howells and Piggott, 1992; Ross and McBean, 1995), and sometimes they are computer based (e.g., see Pear and Novak, 1996). Indeed, there is even one computer-assisted college conducted on PSI lines (Thyer, 1992). This college is described thus:

There are typically no lectures at Walden U[niversity]. Instead, students register for various courses conducted via computer-assisted instruction and proceed at their own pace. A typical courseload consists of four courses each earning 3 hours of credit. The workload is adjusted so that the average student attending six hours per day Monday through Thursday will make timely progress in his/her studies. Once a week students meet in small groups with the professor assigned to each 'course'. The professor reviews the individual's progress, conducts mini-tutorials, and deals with any problems that may arise. All courses are supported through the college's mainframe computer and professors are free to monitor individual student progress each day, if necessary. The courses are structured so that mastery of one lesson plan must be demonstrated prior to proceeding to subsequent material. Adequate supplemental examples are built into each program to allow for sufficient review and exercises without repetition of old material. Past work is kept on record and students are free to stop working on a particular course at any time, and to pick it up when their schedule permits. Weekly printouts of student efforts (time devoted to each course, performance on quizzes, etc.) permit faculty advisors to become aware of academic difficulties early on ... (p. 148)

It is virtually impossible to fail a course at Walden U. At worst the student stops working on a given class for a time and picks it up again, with suitable review, when circumstances permit. Students are not permitted to proceed to advanced coursework until foundation content is successfully completed. When a given course is completed, the student receives a grade of 'A'. (p. 150)

This aspect of the course – where all students gain high grades – causes no difficulty in an institution when each course is based upon the same premise. However, it causes considerable difficulties in institutions where only some courses use a PSI approach.

Indeed, this may be one of the factors that has led to the demise of such courses. It appears, generally speaking, that the enthusiasm for PSI courses now seems to be running out. A second possible explanation for this is that people think that because such courses are behaviourally based they do not encourage independent learning and thinking in their students (e.g., see Biggs, 1996). Many commentators believe that PSI may well be effective at the introductory level but that it does not give a good model of what is meant by higher-level independent learning.

Other examples of applications of behavioural principles of learning may be found in the areas of **programmed learning** and computer-based instruction (see Chapter 6), in classroom management generally (see Wheldall and Glynn, 1989), and in the **behaviour-modification** schemes – including **token economies** – that have been used with both normal and learning-disabled children and adults (see Kazdin, 1994; Yule and Carr, 1987).

Applications of cognitive theory

The principles drawn from cognitive theory are perhaps not as clear-cut as those from behavioural psychology, and are, to some extent, absorbed in common practice. None the less, examples of the application of cognitive theories of learning can be seen in research that examines how prior knowledge affects learning (e.g., see Driver *et al.*, 1994), how different teaching materials can be structured and sequenced (e.g., see Beard and Hartley, 1984) and in studies of how information can be organised and displayed in textbooks, handouts and worksheets (e.g., see Hartley, 1994).

The application that I should like to concentrate on in this section is that of **'problem-based learning'**. I place problem-based learning in this section rather than the next because, although learners have considerable autonomy, the problems they face are teacher determined. Furthermore, the assessment is often done using the standard examinations required for obtaining professional qualifications.

25

As my example, let us consider the problem-based approach to medical education introduced at Case Western Reserve University in the USA in the 1950s and at McMaster University in Canada in the 1960s (see Neufeld and Barrows, 1974). Here, in contrast to many medical programmes at that time – and indeed since – students are assumed from the start to be responsible and motivated adults. They are encouraged to define their own learning goals (within a tutor-presented frame of reference), to select appropriate experiences to achieve these goals and to be responsible for assessing their own learning progress. Students work in small groups together with a tutor, and goals are worked out with the tutor's help. The achievement of these goals is assessed by both the students and the tutor. (The tutor, too, is assessed by the students, and can be replaced if not deemed satisfactory!)

The instruction is largely problem centred, and a wide range of resources is available to help the students achieve their objectives – there are actual patients, live simulations, computer simulations, 'problem boxes' – containing programmed texts, tape/slide instructions, study outlines and notes – and a reference library. One key idea is that students learn that few problems are ever actually solved and that trying to solve one problem opens up many more: thus the notion of sequential learning is abandoned.

This approach to medical education, which seemed astonishing in the 1970s, has become more widespread and subject to considerable study (e.g., see Boud and Feletti, 1991; Vernon and Blake, 1994). Boud and Feletti (1991) suggest that 'the principal idea behind problem-based learning is . . . that the starting point for learning should be a problem, a query or a puzzle that the learner wishes to solve'. Problem-based courses start with problems rather than with an exposition of disciplinary knowledge. As Boud and Feletti put it, 'They move students towards the acquisition of knowledge through a staged sequence of problems presented in context, together with associated learning materials and support from teachers.'

Although there are no universally agreed procedures in problem-based learning, the method is usually characterised by the following features:

- the problems used as stimulus materials are 'real-life' problems;
- these problems typically cross traditional subject-matter boundaries;
- instructions on how to solve the problems are not given, but the resources necessary to solve them are;
- students work together in small groups, with access to an instructor (who is not necessarily an expert in the subject matter) who can facilitate their learning; and
- students typically work on one problem at a time (as opposed to studying, say, four modules per term).

Most research on problem-based learning has been conducted in the medical context. However, Boud and Feletti's textbook contains examples of it in information science, mechanical engineering, optometry, architecture, law, management, economics, and social work. There seem to be few published examples of this approach in psychology, although perhaps the papers by Arnold *et al.* (1994) and O'Connell *et al.* (1995) come close.

Applications from social and phenomenological theory

Applications of social and phenomenological theory are perhaps illustrated in their starkest form in the work of the so-called '**de-schooling**' movement in the 1960s. Goodman, Holt, Illich, Reimer and others have all described how organisational forces acting in the classroom can markedly affect how children learn and teachers teach (see, e.g., Holt, 1982a: Lister, 1974). These authors were in favour of abandoning schools altogether, and allowing children to do what they liked, when they liked, and how they liked. Schooling, they believed, led children to develop a fear of failure and to develop strategies for hiding this from their teachers – strategies that lasted a lifetime. Such behaviours resulted from what was called the '**hidden curriculum**' of schooling – and even of higher education. (Think of why some students don't speak in

27

tutorials . . .). According to some people, strategies for 'beating the system' – and thus not admitting to failure – are rife in university education (see Norton *et al.*, 1996).

Indeed, the debate about 'traditional' versus 'progressive' teaching in primary schools relates to these issues (see Bennett, 1976) and this debate still continues with our present concerns over the National Curriculum and the 'back to basics' approach of some politicians.

At university level there have been a number of attempts to be more 'progressive' and to offer more freedom to students than is normally available. The argument is that such freedom encourages motivation and taking responsibility for one's own learning (Rogers and Freiberg, 1994). These points are relevant to the notion of encouraging students to become life-long learners – an issue I discuss further in later chapters of this book.

In the United Kingdom for several years, Lancaster University, Crewe and Alsager College (now part of Manchester Metropolitan University) and the North East London Polytechnic (now the University of East London) have provided courses that allow students greater freedom than that allowed in most other institutions. At Lancaster, the School for Independent Studies offers an undergraduate degree; at Crewe there is a final-year option and, at East London, there are independent routes to diploma, undergraduate and masters-degree levels.

Brook *et al.* (1994) provide a brief description of Part 1 of the Lancaster Independent Studies course, and they include this extract from the course handbook:

> Based in a supportive small group environment, Independent Studies Part 1 empowers students to take responsibility for their own learning, and explore and develop their academic and personal potential, through flexible learning practices.
>
> The course aims to achieve this by offering the students the opportunity to:
>
> ● benefit from participating in small learning groups;
> ● gain academic and personal confidence, by developing existing and new skills;

- pursue individual interests, and utilise a variety of creative approaches;
- learn through active educational experiences; and
- engage in collaborative study.

The students on the course meet in small groups of (about eight) students with a tutor for two hours per week. In addition, they attend a study-skills workshop. During the three terms they have to produce six pieces of work. This work can take several forms in addition to the usual essays and reports – for example, sculpture, music, drama, poetry – and group work is encouraged. Assessment can be carried out by the tutors, the group or the individual student.

Some data indicating the success of the whole course were published in the 1980s (scc Beard and Hartley, 1984; Percy and Ramsden, 1980). These data suggested that between 1975 and 1980 there were, on average, ten students a year graduating in Independent Studies at Lancaster, with over half of them getting a 2:1 (upper second-class) or a first-class degree. A large proportion of these students were mature ones, perhaps suggesting that this approach was well suited to this type of student at that time.

Similar, more recent, data are reported by Stephenson (1988, 1994) in his accounts of Independent Study at North East London Polytechnic (NELP). Here, as mentioned above, students are able to plan their own programmes of study to diploma, honours-degree and masters-degree levels. Students at NELP have two tutors – a personal one and an academic one – and they plan their programme around particular themes. Stephenson lists the following examples of themes that have been studied:

- the influence of marketing techniques in British politics;
- the role of the word-processor in the primary school;
- automatic control systems in robotics and jetfoil;
- the impact of the World Health Organization special programme on tropical diseases;
- the development of three-dimensional images using print techniques;

- Black children and self-identity in the British school system;
- the computerisation of engineering calculations in oilfield drilling;
- neuroactivity from a biochemical point of view;
- the advent of fibre optics and its impact on society.

According to Stephenson, some of the gains for most students include:

- valuable specialist knowledge and skills;
- a high level of performance;
- a strong sense of personal identity; and
- an increase in self-confidence and self-esteem.

Research papers describing independent study of the kind reported above tend to present a rather rosy picture. It is important to note that the students in these courses have elected to take part. When such courses are arranged so that students are required to participate then not all teachers and all students delight in the prospect (see, e.g., Ertmer *et al.*, 1996; Jordan and Yeomans, 1991; Scott *et al.*, 1997; Stanton, 1988). Part-time and overseas students, in particular, might find such approaches problematic (McDowell, 1993; Purdie and Hattie, 1997).

Concluding remarks

The examples outlined above have shown in extreme form how the principles of learning derived from psychological study can be utilised in educational practice. But, as noted earlier, we have to remind ourselves that many teachers and learners are eclectic, and use different principles from different areas of psychology as appropriate. Some of the key issues and ideas that students and teachers need to consider further in this regard are developed in the following chapters of this book.

Further reading

Holt, J. (1982a) *How Children Learn*, Harmondsworth: Penguin. If you haven't read Holt, then you should – particularly *How Children Learn* or *How Children Fail* (1982b). But you need to consider these books in the light of the strictures raised in Chapter 1.

McGilly, K. (ed.) (1994) *Classroom Lessons: Integrating Cognitive Theory and Classroom Practice*, Cambridge, MA: MIT Press. An example of applications of cognitive psychology to instruction.

Wheldall, K. and Glynn, T. (1989) *Effective Classroom Learning*, Oxford: Blackwell. A readable account of a behavioural approach to teaching and learning in a British context.

Further reading

Chapter 3

Individual differences and learning

I N THIS CHAPTER I provide examples from four areas of study
concerned with individual differences in learning. The examples range from those of fundamental differences between people,
through major ways of thinking, to strategic choices of ways of
learning and, finally, to preferences.

■

This chapter is concerned with differences between individuals
and how they can affect teaching and learning. In a lecture situation, although everyone is different, the lecturer has to proceed
as though everyone is the same – making an occasional acknowl-
edgement to sub-groups in the audience. Yet the opposite
viewpoint – that no two learners are alike – poses equally difficult constraints on teachers. Individuals can really only be catered
for in one-to-one instruction. However, in some situations – in
classrooms and tutorials, for example – tutors can explore (and
exploit) individual differences in ways that, it is to be hoped, will
help all the participants learn.

Table 3.1 lists different kinds of individual differences related
to learning and studying under four headings. These I call:

- fundamental differences – fundamental in the sense that these
  are very hard to alter;
- cognitive styles – these are ways in which different
  individuals characteristically approach different cognitive
  tasks;
- learning strategies – these are ways in which individuals
  more consciously select methods of approach; and

●   preferences – these are less serious ways in which individuals differ.

Research has been conducted with all of the individual differences (and others) that I have listed in Table 3.1. Clearly, in this chapter I do not have sufficient space to cover them all or, indeed, all of the research on any particular one. So I have chosen to discuss one characteristic example from each of the four groups, and to provide (in Table 3.1) references to recent papers on each of the differences listed.

Fundamental differences

As can be seen from the kinds of differences listed in Table 3.1, this first category describes differences that are very hard to change. That being said, of course, although you cannot change things like age and sex, there is much debate about the influences of such variables on learning and studying. At university level, for instance, prior experiences in connection with these two variables are bound to affect how people learn. Here, as a characteristic example of a fundamental difference between people, I shall consider sex differences in intellectual abilities. I shall consider issues connected with age in Chapter 4.

Sex differences in intellectual abilities   In the 1980s the picture that was drawn concerning differences between the sexes in terms of intellectual abilities was relatively clear-cut. Although it was always acknowledged that vast oversimplifications were being made, it was considered that males and females did not differ greatly on intelligence, that boys were better at spatial tasks, and that girls were better at verbal ones. These views were based largely on the influential book written by Maccoby and Jacklin in 1974. This book set out, by reviewing as much of the research literature as possible, to consider the evidence for the views and beliefs that people had about the differences between males and females.

Maccoby and Jacklin's approach was to summarise the known evidence using the tools then available. Since that time

TABLE 3.1 Some examples of individual differences (and related studies)

Fundamental differences
    Age (Sutherland, 1997)
    Culture (McNamara and Harris, 1997)
    Ability (Wong *et al.*, 1995)
    Sex (Hayes and Richardson, 1995)
    Introversion/extraversion (Eysenck and Eysenck, 1985)
    Motivation (Abouserie, 1995)
    Anxiety (Zeidner, 1996)

Cognitive styles and ways of thinking
    Convergent/divergent (Hartley and Greggs, 1997)
    Reflexive/impulsive (Goldman and Flake, 1996)
    Field dependent/independent (Liu and Reed, 1994)
    Visualisers/verbalisers (Kirby, 1993)
    Abstract/concrete/active/reflective (Willcoxson and Prosser, 1996)
    Locus of control (Millar and Irving, 1995)

Learning strategies
    Deep/surface approaches (Sadler-Smith, 1996)
    Serialists/holists (Paterson and Rosbottom, 1995)
    Focusers/scanners (Santostefano, 1985)
    Various study methods (Chalmers and Fuller, 1996)

Preferences
    Prior knowledge and interest (Tobias, 1994)
    Morning/evening persons (Greenwood, 1995)
    Seating positions (Burda and Brooks, 1996)

Note: Jonassen and Grabowski (1993) provide additional references to studies on most of these variables, and Riding and Rayner (1997) provide a recent work on cognitive styles.

the evidence has mushroomed, and newer statistical tools, such as meta-analysis, have become available for handling it. This newer approach has indicated that the conclusions listed above are oversimplifications. Archer (1996) writes, 'Increased quantification . . . brought the realisation that many of the sex differences that had been extensively discussed and argued over were relatively small in terms of overall effect size.' Not only were these effect-sizes seen to be small, but the arguments about interpreting them became more sophisticated. Halpern's (1992) *Sex Differences in Cognitive Abilities* provides a good beginning for readers interested in pursing these issues in more detail.

Archer (1996) goes on to point out that social contexts are important in determining what appear to be sex differences. He cites studies showing that, for example, 'If the *same* task is presented to boys or girls as *either* a measure of needlework *or* of electronics, the effect of the labelling is to reverse the direction of sex difference in the performance' (emphasis added). The significance of this point of view for this particular chapter is to suggest that the differences between the sexes in an academic context – say, in how many men and women students enrol for engineering – are a function of how they perceive engineering, rather than a consequence of biological differences between them.

Many people also think – because there is today less sex-typed socialisation in the home, the school and the media than in the past – that this accounts for the fact that many of the differences that were once found between the sexes on measures of intellectual abilities have now begun to disappear. Halpern (1992) points to the difficulties of drawing such firm conclusions on issues such as these. It is quite likely, for instance, that the people taking part in studies of sex differences at different time periods will also differ in all manner of other ways.

None the less it is true that these recent social changes have had a remarkable affect on the composition of students attending higher education in the UK. Less than twenty years ago, nearly twice as many men as women went to university, and three times as many did postgraduate work. Today the ratios are much more evenly balanced. However, once they are at university, do women do as well as men? And does this vary for different subject matters?

For many years, the achievement of men at university has been slightly more widespread that of women; that is to say, there have been proportionally more men with very good degrees and more men with very poor degrees than women, and that there have been proportionally more women with middle-quality degrees than men. This generalisation is supported by the data shown in Table 3.2, which shows the percentage of full-time men and women students achieving different degree classes in the United Kingdom in 1995. Such findings have been reported in other different, earlier studies, of full-time students by, for example, Rudd (1984) and Davies and Harré (1989). The current findings in Table 3.2 are, therefore, of considerable interest, for they present much the same picture despite the fact that there have been massive changes in the university system in the UK – such as the increase in the number of universities, the increase in the number of students within them, the increase in the number of modular-based systems (as opposed to the old-fashioned 'finals' where the students' degree classes depended almost entirely upon work carried out and examined in the final year) and the increase in the number of women and mature students.

There have, of course, been a variety of explanations proffered for such findings, and the debate can get quite heated (see Clarke, 1988; Rudd, 1988). Some people (e.g., Rudd) prefer to explain such findings at the top end on the basis of differences in intelligence or ability between the two sexes. Others (e.g., Clarke) prefer a more social explanation – looking at issues of

TABLE 3.2 Percentage of full-time men and women students achieving different degree classes in 1995

Full-time	Degree class				
	1st	2:1	2:2	3rd	Pass
Men (N = 104,654)	8	38	37	7	10
Women (N = 106,553)	6	47	36	4	7

Source: Adapted from figures provided by the Higher Education Statistical Agency.

sex discrimination, and how the data differ for different subject combinations. Thus, for example, it appears that there are more first-class degrees in science subjects than in arts subjects and that more men students study the sciences than women (Tomlinson and Macfarlane, 1995).

Indeed, despite the fact that the overall differences in academic performance are very small, there are still vast differences in the distributions of men and women in different subjects. This can be seen in the percentages of men and women in different disciplines at university (see Table 3.3).

TABLE 3.3 Percentage of men and women first-year students starting in different subjects at Keele University in 1996

Subject	% of men	% of women	Total number starting the course
Computer Science	88	12	93
Physics	78	22	37
Philosophy	70	30	71
Music	65	35	34
Earth Sciences	63	37	49
Chemistry	63	37	30
Mathematics	51	49	85
Geography	51	49	132
History	46	54	129
Law	43	57	157
Classics	40	60	67
Modern Languages	38	62	170
English	37	63	163
Biology	25	75	57
Sociology	22	78	121
Psychology	21	79	155
Education	15	85	33
Criminology	9	91	93

Note: These figures may vary slightly from year to year, and sample sizes for some groups are small.

Table 3.4 shows the percentage of full-time men and women students achieving different degree classes in psychology. The results suggest that men and women now perform equally well at the top end of the distribution, but that men perform worse than women at the bottom end.

What, then, are psychologists to make of all this? What are the practical implications? By and large the differences between men and women in terms of degree results are small (see Tables 3.2 and 3.4) and there is a good deal of overlap – rather like there is in height. Many women students are better than many men students, and vice versa. Both sexes confront difficulties, some of which are common, and some of which are specific. Male nurses, for instance, and women computer scientists may confront different – but sex-related – issues (e.g., see Davidson, 1996; Radford and Holdstock, 1995; Thomas, 1988). But the solution must be for people to try to reduce such obstacles for all learners, and not to regard them as insuperable because of presumed differences between the sexes. And, as I shall argue in Chapter 5, as far as students are concerned – male or female, gay or straight – it is more important for them to develop their own skills of learning in different contexts than it is to worry about sex differences.

TABLE 3.4 Percentage of full-time men and women psychology students achieving different degree classes in 1995

Full-time	Degree class				
	1st	*2:1*	*2:2*	*3rd*	*Pass*
Men (N = 1,234)	6	32	40	3	19
Women (N = 4,513)	6	26	52	1	15

Source: Adapted from figures provided by the Higher Education Statistical Agency, courtesy of the Society for Research in Higher Education.

Cognitive styles and ways of thinking

Cognitive styles are perhaps less fundamental than are some of the differences listed in Table 3.1. Reber (1995) defines a cognitive style as 'the characteristic style or manner in which cognitive tasks are approached or handled'. Thus an individual's cognitive style reflects his or her preferred manner of perceiving, remembering and thinking. So, whilst intellectual abilities are primarily concerned with the ability to learn, cognitive styles are primarily concerned with differences in the ways of going about it.

Research suggests that cognitive styles are important variables in two key areas:

1   how students make academic and career choices; and
2   how students learn, how teachers teach, and how these interact.

We shall see both of these issues as we discuss a characteristic example of a cognitive style – that of **convergent** and **divergent** thinking.

Convergent and divergent thinking   In the 1960s there was a growing feeling that typical **intelligence tests** did not measure all aspects of **intelligence**. It was argued, for instance, that such tests only measured what was termed 'convergent thinking'. By this it was meant that respondents were required to find a single correct answer to the problem set: their thinking had, as it were, to focus down – or *converge* – on to the one right answer. The opposite of this approach – which, it was argued, was not measured in conventional intelligence tests – was called 'divergent thinking'. This form of thinking is concerned with the capacity to generate responses, to invent new ones, to explore and expand ideas and, in a word, to *diverge*. Convergent thinking thus demands close reasoning; divergent thinking demands fluency and flexibility.

The implications for learning and instruction in this matter centre on three issues: it seems (1) that students who are good at one kind of thinking may not necessarily be good at the other; (2) that students who are good at one kind of thinking may find themselves doing different subjects from students who are good

41

at the other and (3) that teachers and students may not react well to each other if they do not share the same modes of thinking.

Divergent thinking is usually measured by what are called 'open-ended' tests. Typical items in such tests are *verbal*, such as, 'How many uses can you think of for . . . a brick, a bucket, a paperclip, etc.?' or *non-verbal*, such as 'Draw a picture in the space below to illustrate the title "Zebra Crossing"'. Such tests do not require the respondent to produce one right answer – and thus a problem lies in how to score them. Answers are typically scored in terms of:

- Fluency – this measures an individual's ability to produce a large number of ideas in the time allowed. The number of responses given (excluding those that are nonsensical or inappropriate) are scored.
- Flexibility – this measures the ability to produce a wide variety of responses. Responses are grouped into categories and the flexibility score is the number of different categories used.
- Originality – this measures the ability to generate unusual ideas and is based on the most infrequent responses that occur within the group of individuals being tested.
- Elaboration – this measures the ability to develop and expand initial ideas and is based on the amount of detail that the responses contain.

The results from such tests indicate that there are wide individual differences between people on such measures. Box 3.1 gives some examples from one extreme diverger's answering of a series of different kinds of question reported in a final-year student's psychology project at Keele.

Cognitive styles and academic bias In 1966, Liam Hudson showed, with 'reasonably clever' fourth-, fifth- and sixth-form boys (i.e., 16–18 year olds), that arts specialists tended to score highly on open-ended divergent thinking tests, whereas science specialists tended to do the reverse, and that this difference was 'massively significant'. These findings followed on from work in the United States, particularly that of Getzels and Jackson (1962).

However, because these and other researchers sought – somewhat misleadingly – to equate divergent thinking with creativity and convergent thinking with intelligence, a great deal of controversy ensued. This has continued to the present day (e.g., see Fryer, 1996).

Much of the debate concentrated on the implications of the findings for teaching and learning, and particularly on enhancing creativity at primary and secondary level. None the less, there were some studies that attempted to see how far Hudson's findings about arts and science specialists could be replicated with university students. A recent study in this regard (Hartley and Greggs, 1997) divided students into four groups – those studying arts, those studying arts and social sciences, those studying social sciences and sciences, and those studying science – and all of the students involved completed the four tests listed in Box 3.1. The results showed that there was weak support for the notion that divergent thinking tests would decline along the arts–science continuum, but that when the four groups were collapsed into two – mostly arts and mostly science – then the arts students did score significantly higher than the science students on all three of the verbal tests, but not significantly so on the visual ('circles') test.

Student–teacher interaction   In general, it seems that members of staff react more favourably to convergent than to divergent students. To put it bluntly, teachers find divergent students difficult to deal with, and this may be especially true of teachers who are themselves convergent thinkers. Such teachers don't like guessing or playfulness, but prefer a 'more serious' approach. If, however, divergent thinking does enhance creative output then teachers need to be made aware of this and persuaded to encourage divergent thinking rather than to respond to such thinking with hostility.

This issue of student–teacher interaction raises the question of whether or not a match or a mismatch in cognitive style makes for better learning. Witkin (1976) proposed that individuals matched in cognitive style were likely to get along better because they would have:

BOX 3.1 Examples of responses from the same divergent student to four tests used in the study by Hartley and Greggs (1997)

Test 1 Uses of objects

'Listed below are five everyday objects. Think of as many uses as you can for each. You can be as imaginative as you like: a barrel; a paper clip; a tin of boot polish; a brick; a blanket.'

Example responses from a divergent student:
(barrel) put a drink in it; roll it down a hill; squash someone with it; keep stuff in it; take it apart and use it for firewood; try to get into it and make strange noises so that people think there's a ghost around; try to hide a child in it; use it as a toilet; don't use it – keep it as an ornament; throw it away (not scored – inappropriate answer).

Test 2 Word meanings

'Each of the ten words below has more than one meaning. Write down as many meanings as you can for each word: bit, pink, bolt, pitch, duck, port, fair, sack, fast, teacher.'

Example responses from the same divergent student:
(fair) something that's reasonable; someone with easily burnt skin; someone with blonde hair; somewhere you can ride the waltzers at.

Test 3 Common problems

'Write down as many possible problems that might arise when taking a bath.'

Example responses from the same divergent student:
There might be no water; there might be no bath; there might be no hot water; the bath could be too dirty and you don't have any cleaning agents; you might jump in with all your clothes on; it might be too hot when you

BOX 3.1 Continued

get in, or too cold; the taps don't work; there's a water shortage in the area and taking a bath is forbidden; you might get soap in your eyes; your next-door neighbour might be making loads of noise and taking a bath means irritation because it's right next to your neighbour; someone else might want a bath at the same time; you might drown; you might get soapy water in your mouth (not scored – a repetition); when you get out you might have forgotten your towel, so you have to run to get one and you're wet and naked; all your towels could be dirty; there's no soap or shampoo left; the bath has a crack in it; you can't get in the bath because you are too fat; you could be real tall and get annoyed when a small portion of you seems able to fit underwater; you might not want a bath; there's no bubble bath (not scored – a repetition).

Test 4 Circles test

(Each participant is given a sheet with six rows of five circles drawn on it – all the same size.) 'By using lines, both inside and outside the circles, attempt to make as many different objects as possible. Again you may be as imaginative as you like. If your design is not easily recognisable, you may write a title under each drawing.'

Example responses from the same divergent student:
(All labelled) A bloke, woman, dartboard, spider, brain, beachball, a circular part of Y fronts, face, sun, moon, circle, lollipop, pair of boobs (two circles joined together), balloon, record, odd chair, circular house, someone's foot (not scored – nonsensical), someone's hand (not scored – nonsensical), bird's-eye view of toilet, coin, Scotch video-tape circle, odd-shaped cigarette, a cracked egg, a chick, a dog – woof, woof, bark, a badly drawn lion, a line in a circle (not scored), a square in a circle (not scored).

- Shared foci of interest – individuals with the same cognitive style have a shared tendency to attend to the same aspects of the environment.
- Shared personal characteristics – individuals matched in cognitive style are likely to share similar views, dress in a similar manner and so on.
- Similar modes of communication – individuals with the same cognitive style tend to be on the same 'wavelength' and, for example, use similar non-verbal gestures to accompany speech.

Whether or not a match in cognitive style between student and teacher makes for better student learning is uncertain, as research in this area has produced mixed results. One might argue that a mismatch in cognitive style, providing it is not too great, can benefit student learning. In the case of cognitive styles where a greater value is placed on one end of the dimension than on the other, a teacher with a slightly more positive style than the student may encourage the student to develop in this respect (Hayes and Allinson, 1996).

It is, of course, difficult to carry out studies to assess the effects of matching and mismatching teachers and students on any particular measure. Some such studies have, however, been carried out in the United States, where student class sizes are generally much larger than in the United Kingdom (see, for example, Domino, 1971). However, with the advent of computer-assisted learning (see Chapter 6) we may expect an increase in the number of studies that try to match learning styles to methods of instruction. The following papers illustrate the beginnings of this approach: Kwok and Jones (1995); Liu and Reed (1994); and Paterson and Rosbottom (1995).

Learning strategies

The strategies that learners use to learn and study are – sometimes – more consciously initiated and controlled than are their learning styles. **Learning strategies** are thought to be less general and less fixed. Different strategies are selected by learners to deal with different tasks.

Deep and surface learning   One learning strategy currently receiving much attention is whether or not students adopt a **'deep'** or a **'surface'** approach to studying. Here the story begins in the 1970s. In a series of studies conducted in Sweden, Ferenc Marton and his colleagues asked students how they studied written texts. The replies of the students were categorised either as those of 'deep' or those of 'surface' processors. Deep processors gave replies like: 'I try to get at the principal ideas'; 'I try to find the main points of the chapter'; ' I think about how the author has built up his argument.' Surface processors give replies like: 'I just read straight through from start to finish'; 'I try to concentrate on remembering as much as possible'; 'I didn't remember what I read because I was thinking of hurrying on'. Deep processors, it appears, try to extract meaning from the text: surface processors concentrate on remembering the text itself.

Research has shown that the method of processing that students use has a marked effect upon how well they learn. In one study, Marton and Saljo (1976) asked students to read a 1,400-word article on the topic of curriculum reform in Swedish universities. In the article itself the author had argued that a sweeping reform, aimed at raising university pass rates uniformly, was misguided because different groups of students had different pass rates. The author suggested, therefore, that selective measures should be taken that would concentrate on those particular classes of students that had low pass rates.

After reading the article, the students were asked, 'Try to summarise the article in one or two sentences. What is the author trying to say, in other words?' It was found that the responses could be classified in four ways:

1   Those that reported that there were differences in the pass rates between groups of students.
2   Those that reported that measures were to be taken.
3   Those that reported that different measures should be taken with different groups of students.

4   Those that reported that selective measures should be taken, i.e. only for particular categories of students with low pass rates.

Table 3.5 shows what happened when these replies were analysed with reference to whether or not the students were considered to be deep or surface learners. (This analysis was based on further questioning about how they had read the text.) Clearly, the students' approaches to reading the text had had a marked effect. None of the students labelled 'surface' processors had adequately summarised the main points of the article, whereas none of the students labelled 'deep' processors had failed to do so.

Box 3.2 shows how the answers to an essay examination question might be classified along similar lines.

During the 1980s, several questionnaire measures began to appear that measured deep and surface approaches to studying, and around the world the number of studies mushroomed. One typical questionnaire was Entwistle and Ramsden's (1983) 64-item 'Approaches to Studying Inventory'. This excited great interest, and shorter forms (32-item, 30-item and 18-item) were developed. Box 3.3 provides some typical questions. Much of the research conducted since has focused (1) on the validity and reliability of these and similar questionnaires, and (2) on the relationship between scores obtained on these scales and academic performance (e.g., see Newstead, 1992).

TABLE 3.5 The relationship between 'deep' and 'surface' processing and text understanding

	Level of outcome			
Level of approach	A	B	C	D
Surface	5	8	1	0
Not clear	1	0	6	0
Deep	0	0	4	5

Source: Adapted from Marton and Saljo (1976).

BOX 3.2 Typical approaches of deep and surface learners to an essay examination question

Question: How important are individual differences in learning and studying?

Sample responses – giving a progressively deeper approach:

1   There are four kinds of individual differences: sex differences, convergent and divergent thinking, deep and surface processing, and preferences.

2   In his lecture Hartley described a variety of individual differences in learning and thinking. In this essay I shall discuss four of these – sex differences . . .

3   Hartley described in his lecture a variety of individual differences in learning and thinking which range in importance. In this essay I shall discuss four of these – sex differences . . .

4   Hartley described four kinds of individual differences in learning and thinking which range in importance, and gave an example of each kind. In this essay I shall suggest that whilst this framework forms a useful explanatory device, it is appropriate to concentrate here on the 'fundamental differences' outlined by Hartley. Accordingly, I shall discuss his proffered example – that of sex differences – but I shall also discuss additional examples of what he terms fundamental differences. In doing so, I hope to show that individual differences are, indeed, extremely important considerations in any discussion of learning and studying.

Note: Essays 1 and 2 fail to appreciate the point of the question, and Essays 1, 2 and 3 involve little more than regurgitation of the lecture content. Essay 4, however, involves little, if any, regurgitation, and focuses on the question set. It also demonstrates that the writer has done additional reading in this area. (These sample responses are adapted from actual responses to a similar question set in an examination at Keele in 1996.)

BOX 3.3 Some typical items from questionnaire measures of 'deep' and 'surface' learning. (Students respond on a five-point scale, ranging from strongly agree to strongly disagree.)

Items measuring a 'deep' approach:

I generally put a lot of effort into trying to understand things which initially seem difficult.

I often find myself questioning things that I hear in lectures or read in books.

I usually set out to understand thoroughly the meaning of what I am asked to read.

When tackling a new topic, I often ask myself questions about it which the new information should answer.

Items measuring a 'surface' approach:

Lecturers seem to delight in making the simple truth unnecessarily complicated.

I find that I have to concentrate on memorising a good deal of what we have to learn.

When I am reading I try to memorise important facts that may come in useful later.

I usually don't have time to think about the implications of what I have said.

Source: Items reproduced with permission from Entwistle and Ramsden's (1983) *Understanding Student Learning*, copyright © Croom Helm

Findings, such as those provided in Table 3.5, were replicated in many countries (see Ramsden, 1992). However, more important, some of these studies also showed that students varied their reading strategies (e.g., Laurillard, 1979). Thus the same student might be a surface processor in some conditions and a deep processor in others, depending upon the nature of the task. Such learners were labelled 'strategic'.

In the 1990s, the research began to turn to trying to ascertain what factors might help students to be deep rather than surface processors. Gibbs (1992, p. 9) outlined some of the conditions that encourage *surface* processing as follows:

- a heavy workload
- relatively high class contact hours
- an excessive amount of course material
- a lack of opportunity to pursue subjects in depth
- a lack of choice over subjects, and a lack of choice over the methods of study
- a threatening and anxiety-provoking assessment system.

Some of the teaching strategies that encourage *deep* processing include:

- project work
- learning by doing
- using problem-based learning
- setting assignments that cannot be completed by memory work alone
- using group assignments
- encouraging student reflection
- allowing for independent learning
- providing authentic tasks
- rewarding understanding and penalising reproduction
- involving students in the choice of assessment methods.

I shall continue this discussion of deep, surface and strategic approaches to learning when I discuss study skills in Chapter 5 and assessment in Chapter 7.

Preferences

Preferences are less fixed than learning strategies. They may be deep seated but not of major concern to a particular learner. Here I take seating preferences as my example.

Seating preferences   Most studies of seating preferences, and the effects of different seating arrangements on learning, have taken place in primary and secondary schools rather than in universities. None the less, the findings appear to have some relevance to the latter situation. These findings generally suggest that more discussion takes place if pupils are seated around tables than seated in rows, and that more 'on-task' behaviour occurs when pupils are seated in rows rather than around tables (Hastings *et al.*, 1996).

Figure 3.1 shows a variety of different seating patterns. Feitler and colleagues (1971) reported what happened when university students and teachers were asked to decide which teaching arrangements they would find most comfortable, and which least. The results showed that both students and teachers said that they would feel most comfortable in setting seven. Many of them also picked settings five and two.

Settings one and six were chosen by both teachers and students as being the least comfortable. Despite the general popularity of settings two and seven, many thought that these settings would be uncomfortable for students. The researchers were surprised by the choice of setting six as the least comfortable. It was surprising, they said, because 'the concept of students working in small groups with the teacher helping as needed would appear as one which is desirable and often used, particularly in science laboratory work'. It may be, however, that this result arose from the fact that the schematic diagram did not make clear the flexible role of the teacher (compared with setting two, which was liked by many).

Other studies of seating preferences have suggested that when communication is free:

● the maximum number of communications is made between people sitting opposite each other;

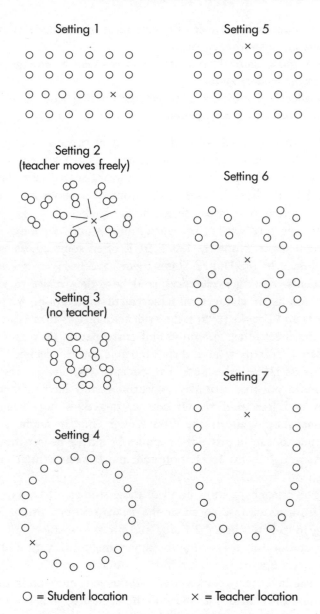

○ = Student location   × = Teacher location

FIGURE 3.1 Some possible seating arrangements *(diagram printed with permission from Psychology Today magazine, copyright © 1971, Sussex Publishers, Inc.)*

- the minimum number of communications is made by people sitting next to each other;
- the most centrally placed person is likely to emerge as the group leader; and
- leaders are most likely to emerge on that side of the table that has the fewest people.

Other studies with schoolchildren seated in rows have suggested that children receive more or less questions from their teachers as a function of the rows in which they are seated (see Hastings *et al.*, 1996). Thus children at the front of a room may receive more questions than those seated at the back.

In a lecture setting, of course, most students choose where they want to sit. None the less there is often some consistency in their choice. In the United States there have been several studies of students' seating preferences, and how they relate to examination results or changes in achievement motivation. According to Burda and Brooks (1996), the evidence suggests that as students sit further back, their attention and participation decreases, their attendance decreases, and their academic grades decline. Burda and Brooks (1996) also note that students who sit near the front have more positive attitudes to learning, and have higher self-esteem and less anxiety. Of course, this does not mean that everyone should sit in the front row(!) but it might suggest that students can improve their grades by sitting nearer the front. (Brooks and Rebeta, 1991, note that more women than men sit in the front rows.)

The crucial question in all of these studies, of course, is do good students choose to sit at the front, or does sitting at the front lead to better grades? Burda and Brooks examined an aspect of this question by measuring the achievement motivation of three different groups of first-year history students seated in different rows. The investigators measured achievement motivation on two occasions: once near the start of the semester, and once again near the end. Data were obtained from students in different classes who had sat in the same seats throughout the course. The scores were pooled to provide data from eighty-nine students who had completed the questionnaires on the first occasion and eighty of them on the second.

Table 3.6 shows the results obtained. It can be seen that students seated in the front two rows had higher achievement-motivation scores on both occasions than the students seated in rows 3 to 4, and 5 to 6. The motivation scores of students in these rows did not differ from each other. Furthermore, it can be seen that the scores at time 2 were higher than the scores at time 1. These overall differences were statistically significant. However, there was no statistically significant interaction between the seating position and the time of the measure. In other words, the increase in achievement-motivation scores from the beginning to the end of the semester was statistically equal for all three pairs of rows. In short, these data support the argument that it was the prior dispositions of the students (in terms of achievement motivation) which led the students to sit in a particular position, and that the class instruction led to an increase in achievement motivation for *all* the students, rather than supporting the view that sitting at the front increased motivation.

TABLE 3.6 Means and standard deviations of achievement-motivation scores for students sitting in the front, middle and back two rows of the classroom, measured near the start and the end of the semester

		Time 1	Time 2
		(N = 89)	(N = 80)
Rows 1 and 2	x̄	12.30	14.18
	s.d.	5.00	5.88
Rows 3 and 4	x̄	8.67	10.96
	s.d.	6.76	6.44
Rows 5 and 6	x̄	8.95	9.65
	s.d.	4.63	6.46

Source: Reproduced with permission from Burda, J. M. and Brooks, C. I. (1996) 'College classroom seating position and changes in achievement motivation over a semester', *Psychological Reports*, 78: 331–336, copyright © Psychological Reports, 1996.

Finally, we should note here that the effects of seating position may be confounded with that of the size of the class. Currently, lecture-group sizes are increasing in the UK, and an issue that is now of key concern is that of the effects of increasing class size on learning. Students interested in pursuing this debate might like to read the reviews by McKeachie (1994) and Gibbs *et al.* (1996) on the effects of class size on learning, and also the study by Perera and Hartley (1997) on the effects of crowding on learning.

Concluding remarks

To conclude this chapter it might be appropriate to comment on the methods that psychologists have used to study individual differences in learning. We have seen that a variety of methods have been used: interviews, questionnaires, qualitative and quantitative studies. Some studies have been quite simple – participants have completed questionnaires and total scores have been correlated with some measure of academic achievement. Or groups have been subdivided on some scale (e.g., of convergence/divergence) and the performance of groups at each end of the scale has been compared, sometimes in different conditions using **analysis of variance**.

More complex studies have administered several questionnaires and tried to work out – using **multiple regression** techniques – which factors are most important in determining success. Wolfe and Johnson (1995), for instance, pooled measures of academic success with those from thirty-two personality variables in trying to predict the academic performance of a group of American psychology students. They found that previous academic success and scores on a measure of locus of control were the most important measures. Other investigators have administered several questionnaires and then used **cluster analysis** to find different 'clusters', or groups of respondents that are similar in some ways but different from other groups (e.g., Entwistle and Brennan, 1971). The advent of computer-based testing, scoring and analysing results may lead to an increase in these kinds of studies. Finally, many investigators have carried out – or reported – meta-analyses (e.g., Halpern, 1992). Today, these rather mechanical – and quantitative – approaches are being supplemented, and indeed sometimes replaced, by more qualitative ones. In studying the academic performance of older students, for instance, there is now a greater willingness to consider case histories and interview data – as we shall see in Chapter 4.

Further reading

Baxter Magolda, M. B. (1992) *Knowing and Reasoning Patterns in Students' Intellectual Development*, San Francisco: Jossey Bass. This text looks at differences between men and women students in terms of how they think and reason.

Eysenck, H. J. (1995) *Genius: The Natural History of Creativity*, Cambridge: Cambridge University Press. A useful review of psychological research in this area.

Halpern, D. E. (1992) *Sex Differences in Cognitive Abilities* (2nd edition), Hillsdale, NJ: Erlbaum. This text conveys in a readable way the complexities of doing research in this area.

Jonassen, D. H. and Grabowski, B. L. (1993) *Handbook of Individual Differences, Learning and Instruction*, Hillsdale, NJ: Erlbaum. If you want to find out what research has been done on any particular individual difference, then this is a good place to start.

Chapter 4

Academic
learning and
older learners

I N THIS CHAPTER I review changes in the ways in which
psychologists are approaching the study of old age and the
implications of this for studying mature students. Data are provided
to show that mature students are little different from traditional-
entry younger ones on most aspects of learning and studying.

■

In the past few years there has been an extraordinary increase in
the number of mature and part-time students in British universities. According to the Department for Education's (1994)
Statistical Bulletin, the number of mature students (defined in
Britain as being 21 years old or older) entering higher education
more than doubled between 1982 and 1992 – and these figures
did not include Open University students. Today, it is claimed,
more mature students enter higher education each year than do
traditional-entry ones, and half of these mature students study on
a part-time basis. Hence the need for this chapter.

Changing views about older learners

The increase in student numbers has been paralleled by a shift in
the attitudes of psychologists in their considerations of how older
people learn. Typically, old age used to be seen as a period of
decline. Although this view still persists to some extent – particularly as regards senior citizens – to hold it today smacks of
'ageism' – or discrimination against older persons.

Psychologists typically consider old age from three perspectives: the *physiological*, the *psychological* and the *social* (e.g., see Bond *et al.*, 1993).

In terms of *physiology*, parts of our bodies start to decline in efficiency from the late teens and early twenties, and continue to decline thereafter (e.g., see Kosnik *et al.*, 1988; Pirkl, 1994). As Table 4.1 shows, these physiological changes are hardly noticeable at first and, indeed, during the middle years people compensate for their deficiencies in various subtle ways so that there is no apparent loss. The behaviour remains the same to the outside observer, but internally, the machinery is working harder, or receiving greater help. Typical methods of compensation for older people involve wearing glasses, turning up the volume of the radio/television, putting brighter light bulbs in the living room, and so on.

Such physiological declines are not likely to affect learning a great deal, although they may do so. I am reminded of one mature student who wrote to me on a feedback form: 'I have great difficulty in reading the reduced-size printing of your handouts. As a psychologist you should know better.'

In terms of *cognition* there has been a considerable shift in the approaches of psychologists. In the 1960s, for example, there was a concern that intellectual capacity appeared to decline with age, and this was attributed to loss of brain function, and various other theories (see Tennant and Pogson, 1995). Both cross-sectional and longitudinal studies appeared to show that people did less well on the various abilities measured by standardised intelligence tests, particularly after the age of fifty or so.

TABLE 4.1 Figures showing the practical effects of declines in eyesight

Age group	Failure rate (%)
Twenties	10
Thirties	10
Forties	13
Fifties	23
Sixties	38
Seventies	62

Note: These data show the UK national failure rates for people in different age groups reading a car number plate at a distance of 20.5 metres.

A distinction can be drawn, however, between **fluid** intelligence (which is concerned with information-*processing* skills) and **crystallised** intelligence (which is concerned with information *storage* of habits or knowledge acquired through the past operation of fluid abilities). Thus it appears that *fluid* intelligence might decline with age, but that *crystallised* intelligence might remain stable, or even increase. The data provided in Table 4.2, for instance, show large increasing age-related declines on tests of perceptual speed and working memory, but not on tests of comprehension and verbal ability.

Another shift in this area of thinking arose, in part, from a recognition of the consequences of using standardised intelligence tests to measure intellectual functioning in old age. Such tests, it was argued, suffered from the fact that (1) they were too culture specific, and (2) they presented problems and tasks derived from the context of schooling rather than from everyday life. Adults, it was argued, might score badly on such tests, but be able to do well on other everyday practical tasks that require a great deal of skill – such as running a business. Indeed, it was reported that, whereas the typical correlations between scores on intelligence tests and academic achievement were of the order of 0.4–0.7 or so, the

TABLE 4.2 Mean scores obtained on different kinds of intelligence test according to age

Age group	Perceptual speed	Working memory	Comprehension	Verbal ability
twenties	40	14	12	30
thirties	40	12	11	31
forties	39	14	11	34
fifties	34	11	12	32
sixties	30	8	10	32
seventies	26	7	10	34

Note: Each age group had seventeen participants, and they completed all the tests.
Source: Adapted from data provided by Zwahr (1998) and reproduced with permission.

correlations between intelligence tests and occupational performance were of the order of 0.2 (Wagner and Sternberg, 1985).

New approaches to intelligence testing thus attempted
to overcome these difficulties. Sternberg's (1985) approach, for
example, assessed analytic, creative and practical skills. And
research workers such as Sherry Willis have also worked with
people of different age groups using tests that measure practical
as well as cognitive intelligence (e.g., see Willis *et al.*, 1992). Thus
today the concern of cognitive psychologists lies not so much
in studying declines in cognitive abilities, but more with ways in
which older people sustain their performance.

In everyday *social* situations older people are faced with the
expectations of their colleagues, friends and family about what
they can and cannot do – to such an extent that these expectations may become self-fulfilling prophecies (Hess, 1994). Adults
are expected to be more socially conservative than teenagers, and
it is often expected that older people cannot adapt as readily to
change as younger ones. The old adage, 'You can't teach an old
dog new tricks', expresses this particular viewpoint well. Indeed,
Coleman (1993) points out, 'a very real problem in our society
is that older people underestimate themselves', and this is despite
the fact that there are some clear illustrations (cited by Coleman)
of where older people learn just as well as, or even better, than
younger ones.

The following two quotations from older learners provide
illustrations of how, for some, these social concerns are apparent.

Quotation 1
'Frequently mature students have problems that they will
not admit to. They don't want to appear thick in front of
their younger counterparts. Instead they plod on trying to
find ways round their problems, often succeeding at the
expense of time, worry and effort.'

Quotation 2
'This situation (lack of sleep from worry) is even more of
a problem for a mature student who lives in a hall of resi-
dence where the other occupants tend to keep later hours

. . . Often students are not satisfied with four hours of punk noise at the Union disco, but decide at midnight to play their stereo or to improvise by kicking a litter bin up the stairs and along the corridor.'

These quotations reflect the notion that older learners will have problems, and the early literature on mature students is replete with this idea. Indeed, in an earlier discussion of what it was like to be a mature student, Ruth Beard and I expressed this point of view quite clearly. We wrote:

Quotation 3
'There is also some debate as to how far *the difficulties* that mature students report concerning learning – of the sort that we have already quoted – really exist, are shared equally with 18-year-olds, or are simply expressions of expectations that these are the issues that mature students should be *worrying* about. As it happens we believe that our quotations reflect genuine *problems*, and we note that Nicholson (1977) considers that the *problems* of mature students are the same as those of younger students, '*only more so*'.'
(Beard and Hartley, 1984, pp. 104–5, italics added)

Today we would be more inclined to agree with the essence of the first sentence in quotation 3 – that it is a matter of debate whether or not mature students have additional problems to those of younger ones. Indeed, one can substitute the words 'young student' for 'mature student' in quotations 1 and 2 above without producing total nonsense. Agreed, older learners might have a range of problems that might not all be experienced by traditional-entry ones, but today many traditional-entry students have financial problems, are single parents, and are forced to attend a local college because their home situation does not permit them to travel to a more prestigious one.

Richardson (1997) and Richardson and King (1997) highlight how most texts discussing older learners concentrate on their difficulties and special needs rather than on their strengths – strengths that come from their greater experience. Richardson and King, for instance, argue that some older learners are likely to have better time-management skills than are traditional-entry ones because they might have been juggling a variety of domestic and occupational responsibilities for many years before they came to university. Indeed, there is evidence to support this proposition. In a recent study, Mark Trueman and I did indeed show that mature students reported a higher use of time-management skills than did traditional-entry ones (Trueman and Hartley, 1996).

Richardson and King go further. In their paper they examined as many studies of mature students as they could find in order to see how they fared compared with traditional-entry ones. In no case did they report mature students being significantly worse than traditional-entry ones, and in many cases they did better. Box 4.1 presents a summary of their results, pooled with those of other investigators who have examined additional features. It can be seen that there is considerable evidence to support a change in thinking about the abilities of mature students.

Academic performance of full-time mature students

One issue that has been examined in detail is the academic performance of mature students compared with that of their traditional-entry cohorts. Studies have been carried out sporadically since the 1970s, and Hartley et al. (1997) were able to summarise the results of eleven British studies in this regard. These authors drew the following broad conclusions from their review:

- mature students usually performed as well as, or sometimes better than, younger ones;
- the results were sometimes affected by the nature of the discipline – with most students, mature or otherwise, doing better in the arts and the social sciences than in the sciences; and
- there were sometimes sex differences in the results, but these were not wholly consistent: often mature women seemed to do better than mature men, but this was not always the case.

BOX 4.1 Summary of the performance of mature and younger students on various measures

Measures of ability

Mature students are broadly similar to younger ones

Measures of study skills

Mature students score better than young ones on measures of:
  deep learning
  time-management

Measures of academic performance

Mature students generally perform as well as, and sometimes better than younger ones

Measures of attitudes to teaching

Mature students are no different from young ones:
  in preferences for different instructional styles
  in conceptions of what constitutes good teaching
Mature students cheat less

There was also some suggestion that older mature students did not do as well academically as younger mature ones, but the evidence for this was weak (Nisbet and Welsh, 1972).

Hartley *et al.* (1997) presented the results shown in Table 4.3 from an archival study of their own at Keele University. It is obvious, by inspection, that there was no significant difference between the performance of mature and traditional-entry students in this inquiry.

It would appear, then, from the results of all these studies taken together, that we can reject the common stereotype that mature students perform less well academically than traditional-entry ones. However, as is usual in psychology, there is a catch.

TABLE 4.3 Distribution of degree classes for 324 traditional-entry and 324 mature students matched in terms of sex and subjects studied

	Degree class					
	1st	*2:1*	*2:2*	*3rd*	*Pass*	*Fail*
Traditional students	16	124	151	26	6	1
Mature students	16	122	139	36	10	1

Source: Hartley *et al.* (1997).

All of the studies described so far were carried out (1) before the then-polytechnics became universities (in 1993–4), (2) before the introduction of 'modularisation', and (3) before 'semesterisation'. Current interest thus now centres on how mature students fare in these new module systems (where each module is examined on its own, and the results are later pooled to arrive at a final degree class).

Mark Trueman and I have carried out one such study with psychology students (see Hartley and Trueman, 1997). In this study we compared the performance of mature and traditional-entry students (matched in terms of sex and other subjects being studied) completing four modules in the first year of the psychology component of their course at Keele University. Modules One and Two comprised lectures and tutorials, and were assessed by an essay and an exam. Modules Three and Four comprised laboratory and statistical classes, and were assessed by laboratory reports. Modules One and Three were taught in the first semester, and Modules Two and Four in the second. The study was first carried out in 1994 and repeated in 1995.

The results obtained for both years showed that the mature students in this study performed equally as well as the traditional-entry students in Modules One and Two, but that the mature students did have greater difficulty than the traditional-entry students with the laboratory and the statistical work in Module Three in the first semester. However, these difficulties had been resolved by the end of Module Four at the end of the second semester. Here both groups performed equally well.

Finally, one additional difficulty needs to be pointed out here. This is that, in all of the studies cited so far, few investigators report on the differences between the mature and the traditional-entry students at the *outset* of their study as well as at the end. Researchers have concentrated on the *end* performance. This means, of course, that we do not really know much about the performance of the two groups over time. It may be, for instance, that at the start of the academic year mature students are poorer academically 'on paper' than traditional-entry ones, and that the end results, which generally show them to be equivalent, are in fact suggesting that the mature students have caught up with, or overtaken, the traditional-entry students. But we do not know. This is a common problem that readers need to look out for when the performance of different groups is being compared: pre- and post-test measures are better than post-test measures alone.

Academic performance of part-time students

The results described above have been obtained with full-time mature students. There are, of course, many part-time mature students (some estimate a quarter of today's student population), but there have been fewer studies of the performance of part-time students in higher education. However, Table 4.4 does provide some recent data that shows the overall performance of part-time students in higher education in 1995. Here the results seem somewhat different from those obtained with full-time and traditional entry students (see Table 3.2 on page 38 in Chapter 3). Clearly part-time students do not do as well as full-time ones – mature or traditional-entry – although the figures are not quite as bad as they initially appear because many part-time students only study for pass degrees.

Perhaps, in this section, we should also include the performance of mature part-time students at the Open University.

TABLE 4.4 Percentage of men and women part-time students achieving different degree classes in 1995

	Degree class				
	1st	2:1	2:2	3rd	Pass
Men (N = 12,519)	6	22	25	8	39
Women (N = 13,327)	5	27	28	7	34

Source: Adapted from figures provided by the Higher Education Statistical Agency.

Clennell (1984) reported data obtained with Open University students in 1982. These showed that their part-time students over 60 years of age (N = 2,800) did in fact do slightly better on average than their part-time students under 60 (N = approximately 62,000) when they were assessed by continuous assessment, but that this difference was reversed in examination conditions. Consequently, there were no overall differences between these two groups when these two different measures were combined.

However, Cohen et al. (1992) failed to replicate Clennell's findings. These investigators found that fewer of their elderly students (aged 61–73) and fewer of their middle-aged ones (aged 41–60) obtained first-class grades compared with their younger ones (aged 25–40) on the cognitive psychology course, D303. Cohen et al. attribute these negative effects of age on academic performance to the peculiarities of D303, and they did not consider them as necessarily contradicting the earlier results reported by Clennell.

Academic performance of 'Access' students

Another area of interest in the UK is how well 'Access' students perform in higher education. (Access students are students – usually mature ones – who enter higher education with few or no traditional-entry qualifications after successfully completing various especially devised one- or two-year 'Access' courses.) Again, figures are hard to come by here. Most studies of Access courses concentrate on evaluating how many students successfully complete the courses, rather than on examining how well such successful students do in their subsequent academic careers (e.g., see Capizzi, 1996).

One exception to this, however, is the paper by Leopold and Osborne (1996). These investigators examined how well students did on an 'in-house' Access course at Stirling University in Scotland, and then how well they did on subsequent modules in degree courses at Stirling. They found that about two-thirds of their students successfully completed the Access course and then went on to study further in the university. In 1993, A grades were given to 6% of the modules completed by these students, B grades to 60% and C grades to 29%. Leopold and Osborne provide data on some twelve or so Access students who finally completed honours or general degrees at Stirling, but the details are rather vague. None the less, the authors conclude that the performance of these students is 'similar to performance in the University as a whole'.

Experiences of older learners

The research findings outlined above have concentrated on what might be termed 'the bottom line' – that is, on final degree performance. However, concentrating on this end result does not help teachers, administrators and students learn much about the qualitative differences between students – mature or otherwise. Individual students may arrive at the same final degree class by a variety of routes, and simply examining degree results does not enable us to differentiate between students with vastly different background experiences and reasons for studying. And there is no doubt that these experiences and reasons for studying do differ (see Box 4.2). This may possibly explain why, if their study habits are superior, mature students do not do better than traditional-entry students in examinations.

BOX 4.2 The diversity of mature women students' reasons for returning to higher education

- I'm 32 now and I've perhaps nearly another thirty years of work . . . I suppose I did in a sense feel that I should do something with my life.
- When the children were both at an age when I could go into education I did. I'd thought about doing it for a long time.
- I think that the main thing was that my husband went out and had an affair – there was absolutely nothing I could do about it – I had no money – then I felt I didn't have any prospects of getting a job other than a factory job – I had two small children – living out in the middle of nowhere – and I was extremely outraged – so I decided then that I was going to work but there was nothing around.
- Only having O levels I couldn't go on to nurse teaching or health visiting because you need educational qualifications. You see these were the only two aspects of nursing that I felt that I wanted to pursue, so I decided to do education full time . . . still with a view to doing these courses and staying in nursing.
- I've always had in the back of my mind that I did need to become potentially independent . . . especially coming towards 50 . . . I felt that if I could stand on my own two feet then I would be doing everybody, including my family, a service.
- I'd always wanted to go back because I . . . I stopped because I was pregnant. I stopped half-way through the course.

Source: Examples reproduced with permission from Pascall and Cox (1993) and the Open University Press.

Four kinds of studies have examined the experiences of mature students. These have been studies that:

1   utilise questionnaires (e.g., Thacker and Novak, 1991);
2   supplement questionnaires with interview studies (e.g., Slotnick *et al.*, 1993);
3   rely solely on interviews (e.g., King, 1994; Pascall and Cox, 1993); and
4   provide case-history accounts (e.g., Arksey *et al.*, 1994).

Let us examine here an example of each.

Questionnaire studies   Thacker and Novak (1991) report a study in which they sent out 416 questionnaires to all of the first-year women aged between 35 and 64 years of age studying at a Canadian university. The response rate was 66%. Respondents were then placed in one of two groups – one with respondents aged between 35 and 44 ($N = 174$) and one with respondents aged between 45 and 64 ($N = 84$). The questionnaire measured a good deal of background information but focused mainly on why the women had come to the university, how coming there had affected them, and what means of support they used to help them in their new situation. Thacker and Novak found that the older women tended to have a higher family income than the younger ones, and they felt less pressure to advance at work or to find a new career. Relatedly, they found that the younger women were more strained in their roles, more pressed by their children's demands, and more pressed for time. The younger women also appeared to have fewer supports to help them cope with the stresses of university. Thus each group had different motives for going to university, different stresses and strains during their first academic year, and used different methods and resources to cope with the demands of student life.

Questionnaires and interviews   In an American study, Slotnick *et al.* (1993) administered questionnaires to nearly 10,000 students attending the University of North Dakota. The sample was divided into a young group – aged 24 and younger – and an older group – aged 25 and older. In addition, these two groups were both subdivided into undergraduate students, postgraduate students, and a professional group (students studying law or medicine). The response rate was 69%. Finally, six members of the younger group and seven members of the older group were interviewed concerning their views on the responses obtained to the questionnaires. Their comments are used throughout the report to personalise the statistics.

Slotnick *et al.* found a variety of things. It appeared that there were no differences in preferred instructional styles for the two groups, and that suggesting that one method of instruction was more appropriate for one group rather than the other was 'ill-advised'. Students in both groups preferred activities that involved them (such as project work) over activities that did not (such as seminars where students were required to present papers and discuss them). Students in both groups did not differ in their conceptions of good teachers and good teaching – although the younger students placed a greater emphasis on the caring nature of a good teacher. In addition, issues of time, money and balancing the various demands of their lives were more of a challenge to the older students. The main conclusion, however, appeared to be that chronological age was not the key variable: rather it was the life and educational experiences of all the students, and their expectations, that mattered.

Interview studies Pascall and Cox (1993) carried out interviews with forty-three women returning to higher education in the UK at the end of the 1970s or the beginning of the 1980s. The interviews were held in 1983–4, and then again eight years later in 1991–2 with a reduced sample of twenty-three of the initial respondents. The initial sample contained fourteen women in their twenties, twenty in their thirties and nine in their forties. In all cases the interviews, which were tape-recorded, were fairly structured and 'sought to elicit information about attitudes and feelings upon leaving school, experiences of marriage, motherhood, work and housework; the decision to return to education; and the expectations and experience of higher education itself'. The results are difficult to summarise numerically, since no (or little) quantitative analyses were employed, although there are numerous quotations. What emerges is a rich picture of the factors that caused these women to return to higher education, and what they felt about it whilst it was in progress, as well as afterwards. However, there are no accounts of actual learning situations of the kind described in the above studies.

Case histories and autobiographical accounts Arksey *et al.* (1994) were mature students themselves when they collected short autobiographical accounts from nine mature students (four men and five women) studying at Lancaster University. Each account describes one particular issue (e.g., 'a day in the life of a mature student') but each is followed by 'other voices' commenting on this same issue. These 'other voices' illustrate the diversity between students, as they all speak differently about the same issue being discussed. In addition, there are one-paragraph descriptions of why each of the nine students decided to take up higher education. Arksey *et al.* conclude that 'there is no common denominator in mature students' experiences'. They consider, however, that mature students do seem to have 'other lives' always present with them – such as activities involving children, partners, elderly relatives and pets – more so than do traditional-entry students – although there are no interviews with students in this latter category.

Concluding remarks

The four kinds of studies described above have produced informative results that flesh out the data obtained from simply reporting on examination results. Few of these studies, however, compare older learners with traditional-entry students: most concentrate solely on mature students. There is a danger, therefore, that stereotypical views about the difficulties of older learners might prevail.

Of course, the labels 'mature' and 'part-time' are far too broad, taking in as they do all students over the age of 21 and contrasting them with 18–20 year olds. We have already seen in

Box 4.2 that there are large differences between students and their reasons for study. Beaty *et al.* (1997) take this further and provide a useful table in this respect. They suggest that students come to higher education for the following four main reasons:

- vocational – to obtain a qualification;
- academic – to acquire academic skills;
- personal – to develop themselves as people;
- social – to pass the time.

Table 4.5 expands on these issues.

TABLE 4.5 The main reasons why students enter higher education

Orientation	Interest	Aim	Concerns
Vocational	Intrinsic	Training	Relevance of course to future career
	Extrinsic	Qualification	Recognition of worth of qualification
Academic	Intrinsic	Following intellectual interest	Room to choose stimulating lectures
	Extrinsic	Educational progression	Grades, academic progress
Personal	Intrinsic	Broadening or self-improvement	Challenge,
	Extrinsic	Compensation or proof of capability	Passing course, feedback
Social	Extrinsic	Having a good time	Facilities for sport and social activities

Source: Reproduced with permission from Beaty *et al.* (1997) and the Scottish Academic Press.

As far as research on older learners is concerned then, what seems to be required are both quantitative and qualitative studies that look at students who differ in their orientations (e.g., those who come for vocational versus those who come for academic and those who come for personal reasons), possibly subdivided into men and women, and in, say, three age groups – e.g., 18–24, 30–40, and over 45. Such studies might be able to map out the particular concerns of these different groups of students, and to see how university teachers and administrators could best help each group.

Further reading

Arksey, H., Marchant, I. and Simmill, C. (eds) (1994) *Juggling for a Degree: Mature Students' Experience of University Life*, University of Lancaster: Unit for Innovation in Higher Education. An easy-to-read set of case histories of nine mature students studying at Lancaster University. Includes some tongue-in-cheek advice.

Bourner, T. and Race, P. (1990) *How to Win as a Part-Time Student*, London: Kogan Page; and Rickards, T. (1992) *How to Win as a Mature Student*, London: Kogan Page. Standard advice manuals covering a range of issues and practical advice.

Slotnick, H. B., Pelton, M. H., Fuller, M. L. and Tabor, L. (1993) *Adult Learners on Campus*, London: Taylor & Francis. Although this exemplary study is American, the issues discussed are very relevant to the UK. For psychology students there is a useful appendix on methodology.

Sutherland, P. (ed.) (1997) *Adult Learning: A Reader*, London: Kogan Page. An up-to-date compendium of research on a wider range of issues connected with adult learning than those discussed in this chapter.

Improving
study skills

I N THIS CHAPTER I first examine traditional research on note-taking and essay writing before moving on to consider how changing conceptions of teaching and learning are altering the ways in which these skills are now studied by psychologists. I conclude with a brief comment on how new teaching methods might increase transferable and life-long skills.

■

If you examine any book on study skills – of which there are many – you will find that there is considerable overlap in the topics covered. Most books on study skills discuss, for example, notetaking, essay writing and preparing for examinations. In addition, there is often discussion of topics like time-management and library skills. However, much of this discussion is based upon the tacit knowledge of the authors and little of it upon actual research. And, partly for this reason, you will find conflicting advice if you look at how different authors handle these different topics.

Psychologists, of course, are interested in the evidence that might support – or reject – these different points of view. In the first part of this chapter I shall consider the traditional sorts of evidence that psychologists have obtained concerning two topics – notetaking and essay writing – in order to illustrate the early contribution of psychologists in this field. (Readers interested in research on other study skills issues might like to consult the references given in Table 5.1.) In subsequent parts of the chapter I shall look at how research on deep and surface learning, and

TABLE 5.1 References to research on issues typically discussed in study manuals

Essay writing	(see the text)
Examination skills	Wark and Flippo (1991)
Library skills	Risko *et al.* (1991)
Listening skills	Bostrom (1990)
Notetaking	(see the text)
Outlining/underlining	Caverly and Orlando (1991)
Presentation skills	Colman (1996)
Reading skills	Girden (1996)
Revision practices	Entwistle and Entwistle (1991)
Self-questioning	King (1992)
Thinking skills	Halpern (1996)
Time-management	Trueman and Hartley (1996)

changes in **conceptions of teaching and learning** are affecting today's research on study skills.

Research on notetaking and essay writing

Notetaking Notetaking has been the subject of much research, beginning at least as early as 1910 and continuing to the present day. Anderson and Armbruster (1991) and Caverly and Orlando (1991) provide reviews of studies of notetaking *from lectures* and notetaking *from textbooks*, respectively. Much of this research has focused on the question of the effectiveness of notetaking in general, but there has been very little research on the effectiveness of training in different notetaking strategies. Indeed, it is surprising, as so many people take notes in different contexts, that there is hardly any research at all on what might be called the qualities of 'good' notes (but see Peck and Hannafin, 1983).

Studies of notetaking in lectures have found that students express two main reasons for notetaking – apart from relieving boredom. Students believe (1) that the process of taking

TABLE 5.2 Findings of early studies concerned with the effectiveness of notetaking

	Number of studies indicating that the process of notetaking aids recall	Number of studies indicating that reviewing one's own notes aids recall
Yes	34	22
No effect	19	6
No	4	0

Source: Based on Hartley (1983).

notes – actually writing things down – will help them to remember the content; and (2) that the product of their labours – the actual notes that they take away – will be useful reminders of what was covered in the course, and will aid subsequent revision. Table 5.2 summarises the evidence that supports these beliefs – assessed in over fifty studies of notetaking. It can be seen that there is considerable support for the view that reviewing notes aids recall, and that there is also support for the notion that taking notes itself aids recall, but that this support is not quite so clear.

In addition to the experimental studies listed in Table 5.2 there were a fair number of studies (about twenty or so) which examined relationships between what was noted (usually measured in a word count) and what was subsequently recalled. The results here tended to show moderate positive correlations (of the order of +0.20 to +0.50) between the amount noted and the amount recalled.

The overall conclusion to be drawn from this early research, then, seems to be that there is evidence to suggest that notetaking helps people to remember information. However, before arriving quite so firmly at this conclusion, we might first want to be somewhat critical of the research methods that have been used in determining it. Some limitations have been as follows:

● In nearly all of the studies reviewed the students knew that they were taking part in experiments on notetaking: this could have affected their behaviour.

- In such experiments students who habitually took notes might – by chance – have been instructed not to take notes and, correspondingly, students who normally did not take notes might have been instructed to do so: therefore their normal behaviour might have been distorted.

- Few of the studies considered the relevance of the 'lecture' given for the students involved. Some 'lectures' contained fictitious or remote material, and some were tape-recordings of very short passages.

- Almost all of the studies assumed that measuring the amount retained on a test after a period of time was the appropriate (and only) measure to use: such an approach does not consider other outcomes of notetaking.

- Most of the studies utilised only one lecture situation – so that any variability in notetaking due to differences between topics, lecturers and other factors, such as experience, was ignored.

- Few of the studies examined what the students did with their notes between taking them and revising from them.

In short, these early studies suffered from a lack of 'ecological validity' – that is to say, they were experimental in nature, and not very realistic in practice.

Subsequent research in the 1980s attempted to overcome these problems. Then it became more typical to have studies where:

- The students were not aware that a study on notetaking was taking place.

- The topic of the lecture was one from a current series, and the topic was to be examined later, so the lecture content was relevant to the students.

- Information was gathered on what the students had done with their lecture notes since taking them.

- Other measures of study activities, as well as notetaking, were considered when examining examination results.

In short, this later research on notetaking was more authentic.

Illustrations of this latter approach can be found in the papers by Norton and Hartley (1986) and Nye *et al.* (1984). Norton and Hartley examined examination scripts in detail to see if it was possible to locate the sources of the material used. The students involved had attended a lecture on the topic examined (programmed learning), received a lecture handout, and taken notes without being aware that an experiment was in progress. The notes had been handed in at the end of the lecture, photocopied and returned. In addition, the students had been recommended to read a relevant article (placed on reserve in the library), and a chapter in the course textbook.

It was possible, by careful and assiduous reading of each sentence of the examination scripts, to determine whether or not any of these four sources (notes, handout, article and chapter) figured in the examination answers – together with two further, less-specific sources: 'additional reading' – supported by references, and 'untraceable'. It appeared that the course textbook was the most widely used source (approximately 70% of the students referred to it), with the article on reserve next (over 50%). Some 35% used their lecture notes and some 20% the lecture handout. Three-quarters of the students appeared to have done some additional reading and there was much material whose source was untraceable.

Further analyses showed that the more sources a student used in answering the examination question, the higher the mark obtained. In addition, some sources contributed more to this mark than did others. Thus a student using one particular source rather than another might have received higher or lower marks. In this case the most useful sources for the students appeared to be the article on reserve, followed by the students' own notes. After this it was not possible to distinguish between the remaining sources in terms of their importance for the examination answer.

This study illustrates a more naturalistic and realistic approach to the topic and shows that notetaking combines with other study skills in aiding learning. However, like all studies, this one has its limitations. Here the person who (1) gave the lecture, (2) produced the handout, (3) wrote the article on reserve, and

(4) marked the examination papers was one and the same person. It would have been better, of course, to have had the examination scripts marked by independent judges, and perhaps to have had an article written by someone else placed on reserve.

Finally, some other, more recent work, on notetaking is of interest here in that it shows how students reviewing their notes in pairs do better in tests of subsequent recall than students reviewing them individually (Kelly and O'Donnell, 1994; O'Donnell and Dansereau, 1994).

Essay writing   Psychologists have used a variety of approaches in studying how students write essays. These have ranged from observing students writing, examining students' accounts, using interviews and questionnaires, and analysing the features of successful essays. The focus of attention in traditional studies of essay writing seems to be on assessing the evidence for the usefulness of the various strategies that essay writers employ.

Box 5.1 shows the data that I once obtained with a rough-and-ready questionnaire at Keele with second-year psychology students in the 1980s – before the advent of word-processing. (The effects of word-processing on essay writing will be discussed below, and in Chapter 6.) A similar questionnaire was used by Branthwaite *et al.* (1980) in their research. In this study the authors provided a picture of what students said they did, and they also tried to relate their responses to the essay marks obtained. What was of interest in this particular exercise was the fact that Branthwaite *et al.* were unable to relate the use of any of the strategies independently to the essay marks (with the exception of allowing time for reflection between reading and starting to write). Thus it did not seem to matter much whether or not a student said 'yes' or 'no' to a particular question in terms of the examination mark obtained. Furthermore, the authors were unable to come up with any groups of items that, if an individual agreed to all of them, would produce a higher mark.

What Branthwaite *et al.* did find, however, was surprising. They were able to relate essay-writing strategies to experience – or to year of study. They found, for instance, that they could tell – with a 95% level of accuracy – from the pattern of responses to the questionnaire items whether or not the respondent was a first-year, second-year or third-year student on Keele's four-year course. It appeared that students in their first year worked hard, and they did the 'right' things, but that they were not very confident or enterprising. Thus they allocated more time, used the recommended books and worked on one essay at a time. Students in their second year did not work so hard, but were

BOX 5.1 Results from a questionnaire on essay writing with second-year psychology students at Keele University in the mid-1980s. (N = 90: 33 men and 57 women)

Questions

How long before handing an essay in do you start work on it?

	Men	Women
1 day	–	–
2–3 days	–	1
4–7 days	10	16
1–2 weeks	11	19
2–3 weeks	8	11
3+ weeks	4	10

In preparing for an essay do you:	[% agreement] Men	Women
1 Allocate in advance certain times for this work?	39	63
2 Read books, articles (not necessarily all the way through)?	100	100
If so, roughly how many? (i) books	2–8	1–10
(ii) articles	0–5	0–10
3 Use lecture notes and handouts?	88	74
4 Use books/articles other than those recommended by the tutors in the course programme?	88	91
5 Draw up a time-table for the work?	12	16

more confident. They read more books, especially *not* recommended ones, looked for existing essays on the topic written by previous students and discussed what they were writing with other students. The few students. in their third year (who were retaking the course) did not work very hard, were pessimistic and far from enterprising.

Norton (1990) provides a good exemplar for studies that look for features in essays that lead to good marks. She, too, used a questionnaire – which is reprinted in her paper – and, in addition, she interviewed six of the essay-markers. Norton found that

BOX 5.1 Continued

	[% agreement]	
	Men	Women
6 Leave time for reflection between finishing the reading for the essay and starting the essay?	58	51
7 Make a written plan of the essay structure?	61	86
8 Make a draft of the essay, and then write up the essay? If so, how many drafts?	Median 1 Range 0–3	Median 1 Range 0–4
9 Discuss your plans with someone else?	36	33
10 Give the essay to someone else to read before handing it in?	18	9
11 Rewrite and reorganise notes made from lectures, books, articles before writing them into the essay?	73	68
12 Try to draw your own conclusions and present your own ideas?	94	86
13 Find it necessary to fill out the essay to make it longer?	24	21
14 Only work on one essay at a time?	76	81
15 Look around for existing essays on the same topic?	36	26

the following three features of essays were significantly associated with good results:

- Time spent: students who spent more than seven hours on the essay did better than those who spent less than this.
- Length: there was a correlation of the order of +0.63 between length of the essay and the mark awarded.
- Number of references: the more references, the higher the mark.

There were additional features – like planning and the number of sources used – that seemed helpful, but these were not statistically significant features. Broadly similar results were found by Mahalaski (1992) in an interview study with geography students and their tutors.

Generally speaking, the literature on essay writing is, like the literature on notetaking, largely advisory in nature. The authors of study manuals exhort students to do certain things in order to obtain a good mark. Mahalaski's study shows that much – but not all – of this advice is useful.

Indeed, there appears to be three main things that study manuals advise when it comes to writing essays: (1) that students should plan their essays in advance; (2) that they should write clearly and simply; and (3) that they should revise their initial drafts.

Actually, when it comes to looking at the research evidence, there is very little to support the value of planning as a major determinant of essay marks, despite the fact that 70% of students typically say that they plan (when responding to questionnaires). The problem here is perhaps what is meant by planning. Some useful discussions on what is involved in planning are provided in the interview studies of Hounsell (1997) and Mahalaski (1992). Studies currently in progress at Birmingham University with psychology undergraduates suggest that students can be grouped into three different kinds of essay writers:

- *outliners and drafters*: these students typically write a full outline and follow this by writing one or two drafts;

- *drafters*: these students typically write two or more drafts, but do not write full outlines. They may use mental and/or rough notes, however;
- *single drafters*: these students typically produce a single draft which is then corrected for minor errors.

However, not all of these students are consistent over time (in this case three years). And, as found in earlier research, these different strategies are not related clearly to the essay marks awarded (Torrance *et al.*, 1997).

It is easy to exhort students to write clearly and simply but it is not actually easy to do it. The advice given in general study manuals largely ignores the fact that students are expected to write within certain conventions – and that different disciplines have different conventions. More specific study-skills books are thus more useful in this respect (see, e.g., Smyth's 1996 text on writing in psychology).

Rewriting, and redrafting, of course, are major problems with writing essays by hand or with a typewriter. Word-processors, of course, greatly facilitate these processes. Editing with a word-processor allows one to check separately for (1) errors in spelling and punctuation, (2) the consistent use of headings and layout style, and for (3) the appropriate presentation of references in the text and subsequent reference list. There is some evidence that people plan less and revise more when they are using word-processors than they do when they are writing essays by hand, but this evidence is not conclusive (see Chapter 6). It is possible that this additional revision may lead to essays written on a word-processor getting higher marks than those written by hand (Oliver and Kerr, 1993) but Torrance *et al.* (1994) found no relationships between the use of word-processors and essay marks obtained by psychology students.

Changing conceptions of teaching and learning

I outlined in Chapter 3 how – in the section on learning strategies – the distinction between 'deep' and 'surface' learners had developed. Indeed, this distinction now dominates much of the research in learning and instruction around the world, although it is less common in North America than in Europe.

But the issues have got more complex. In parallel with the interest in deep and surface learning an interest has also developed in what is often called students' 'conceptions of learning'. And these two interests are interrelated – as we shall see.

The starting point for research on students' conceptions of learning begins in the United States with studies by William Perry in the 1960s and 1970s (Hofer and Pintrich, 1997). Using interview and questionnaire studies with students from Harvard and Radcliffe, Perry described a nine-stage progression in how students thought about what learning was, and what it involved. These stages progressed from an *absolutist* point of view (in which knowledge was seen as right or wrong, good or bad, and handed down by an authority figure) to a *relativistic* one (that recognised the flexibility of knowledge and the possibility that it could be questioned through reasoning). Table 5.3 encapsulates Perry's model (reduced to five stages). Clearly, students in stages 1 and 2 are very different from students in stage 5.

Later European interview work – for example, that by Saljo (1979) – also distinguished between five different conceptions of learning held by students when they were asked to explain what they meant by learning. These conceptions – following Saljo (1979) – are:

1 *Learning as a quantitative increase in knowledge*
Learning involves acquiring information, or 'knowing a lot'.
2 *Learning as memorising*
Learning involves storing information that is later reproduced.
3 *Learning as acquiring facts, skills and methods*
Learning involves remembering knowledge and procedures that are going to be useful at a later date.
4 *Learning as making sense, or as abstracting meaning*
Learning is a process, and the nature of what is learned is changed. Learning is a constructive activity.

TABLE 5.6 Perry's model of conceptions of learning

View towards	Perry's scale 1–2	3	4	5
Knowledge	All knowledge is known	Most is known but there are some fuzzy areas	Some is known; no certainty; anything goes	Different knowledge is needed in different contexts
Answers to problems	Either right or wrong		My answer is as good as yours	No absolute truth; answers are relative but good answers exist once the conditions are known
Teacher, tutor, instructor	Instructor and books know the truth	Role is to tell us how to learn	Role is as models; but they can be completely discounted	Role is to be a guide and source of expertise
Student's role	To receive	To work hard and to learn how to learn	To think for yourself; independent thought is good	To identify the conditions; to choose the best ideas
Assessment	Worried if exam format is fuzzy. Asks 'What do you expect?' Equates bad grades with bad person	Is the key issue. Quantity and fairness. Hard work = good mark	Independent ideas equal good mark. Can separate assessment of work from personal worth	Seek positive and negative feedback on assessment
Preferred task	Memorise definitions	Compare and contrast	Analysis	Synthesis. Relate ideas between contexts
Difficult task	Decide which of two conflicting authorities is correct. Tell me	Focus on the 'process' and not on the answer	Provide evidence to support claims. Learning to listen to authority again	Decide on which conditions apply

Source: Adapted from Perry (1970), reproduced with permission.

5   *Learning as a process that helps us to interpret and under-stand reality*
Learning involves comprehending the world by reinter-preting information and knowledge in the light of one's own experience and values.

It is not difficult to see how these different conceptions of learning relate to deep and surface processing. It is clear that the first two are concerned with learning as memorising and repro-ducing information verbatim, whereas the last two are concerned with constructing personal meaning. But the point to emphasise here is that students who hold different conceptions of learning will perceive what is being said and taught in their classes in different ways.

Finally, we need to note that students' conceptions of learning are related to their conceptions of teaching. Students who believe that learning involves memorising are likely to appreciate teachers who give them factual information and clear instructions. Students who believe that learning involves understanding and making meaning out of information are likely to appreciate teachers who involve them more in the learning process and who are less direc-tive. Thus students (and teachers) have conceptions of learning and teaching, all of which may vary in different teaching situations.

Furthermore, students (and teachers) may change with ex-perience: students may shift from being surface learners at the beginning of their first year to deep ones at the end of their final year (although the evidence for this is weak: see Nulty and Barrett, 1996; Ramsden and Entwistle, 1981; Watkins and Hattie, 1981).

Today student learning is often characterised in the kind of diagram shown in Figure 5.1. This model assumes that a key feature in learning is the perception by the student and the teacher of the context in which the learning takes place. However, some investigators go so far as to say that in these situations 'the tail wags the dog'. Thus if students perceive that surface learning is all that is required to obtain a good grade, then this perception will drive their approach, and their perceptions of the teacher and the learning situation. In short, the apparent directional flow of the diagram can be reversed.

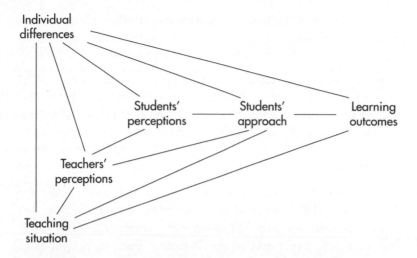

FIGURE 5.1 Model of the relationships among student, teacher and learning outcomes *(adapted from figures provided in articles by Biggs and Gibbs in Smith and Brown, 1995)*

New approaches to improving study skills

This section of this chapter is divided into two parts. First, I shall return to the topics of notetaking and essay writing in order to show how these more modern approaches take into account the issues discussed above. Then I shall comment on teaching methods designed to encourage deeper processing in students.

Notetaking revisited There have been few attempts to describe how deep and surface processors, or students with different conceptions of learning, might differ in their notetaking strategies. Possibly this is because notetaking, particularly in many lectures, can hardly be judged to be a 'deep' activity. It is what one does with the notes that matters. (The studies with paired learners mentioned earlier by Kelly and O'Donnell, 1994, and O'Donnell and Dansereau, 1994, are thus of particular interest in this respect.)

Morgan (1993), however, does illustrate through quotations how deep and surface processors tackled notetaking from a correspondence text. One student writes, for example:

> I have a quick look and see how long I am going to take on it then I just read straight through and use the felt tip pen . . . I ring various theories as I go through it and I make a few notes on small index cards on what the various theories are . . . What I tend to put down are the main points in each block.

Morgan characterises this response as that of a student at stage 4 in Saljo's (1979) classification described earlier (p. 88). The student is searching after meaning, but is not involved in translating this into a personal matter. However, this can be contrasted with another response:

> I have been writing what I consider to be quite a lot of notes. This time the only notes that I have really taken are to do with the written assignment. I have taken some notes on that, but the rest I have been putting on audiotape, which I am trying to learn . . . I think it comes over better, you know, getting it on an oral basis rather than reading it all the way through because a lot of these notes were just a matter of sheer copying from the unit (correspondence teaching text).

This response might be characterised as that of a student at stage 2 in Saljo's analysis, with its emphasis on copying and memorising.

In addition, rather more detailed interview studies, of the kind conducted by Van Meter et al. (1994), are also of interest here. This study shows clearly how students adapt their notetaking strategies according to (1) their goals, (2) how relevant they perceive the material to be, (3) their own background knowledge and experience, (4) their conceptions of learning, and (5) the presentation style of the lecturer. This richer description of what is involved in notetaking now needs to be fed forward into the guidance given in study manuals.

Essay writing revisited   There have been few studies of how students write essays in the context of students' conceptions of learning. Using interview data, Biggs (1988), however, discussed the kinds of essays written by students of English who varied on the deep-surface dimension. Biggs examined the approaches of different students in terms of their approaches to the task, their planning of the presentation of the essay (the content, the sequencing, etc.), and their actual writing strategies in producing it. Table 5.4 presents a selection of responses from deep and surface learners in these regards. Similar quotations can also be found in the study by Prosser and Webb (1994) with sociology students.

Finally, in this section, may I remind the reader of Box 3.2 (p. 49). Here these different essay examination answers may also be characterised in terms of different conceptions of learning.

Teaching methods and deep and surface learning   It appears that developing students' learning skills involves rather more than just running traditional study-skills courses (Kaldeway and Korthagen, 1995). So investigators have started to experiment with new teaching methods in order to encourage deeper learning in their students. There are several examples of such an approach in various subject matters (e.g., see Gibbs, 1992, 1994, 1995, 1996; Rust and Gibbs, 1997). The studies by Baillie *et al.* (1996), Cuthbert (1995), and Norton and Crowley (1995) provide examples from psychology – as well as references to studies in other disciplines.

Norton and Crowley (1995) attempted to improve the quality of their psychology students' learning by integrating eight workshops into their first-year course. Attendance was strongly encouraged but was not compulsory. The topics of the workshops (and the numbers attending) are shown in Table 5.5.

All the students who attended the first and penultimate workshops were asked to write as much or as little as they wanted on the question, 'What do you actually mean by learning?' The answers were classified in terms of one of the five conceptions of learning described above (p. 88). At the end of the course, data were collected on the students' coursework marks (mean essay grade for two essays) and their end-of-year examination marks.

TABLE 5.4 How deep and surface learners write essays

Approaches to the task

Deep: 'I like to get into things a lot more deeply than I should. That's my problem. I've got to stop myself getting too engrossed in it . . . I hope to get an "A". Actually, I'd like to get an "A+".'

Surface: 'I just write to get it finished . . . because I've got to write it . . . I'll be lucky if I pass . . . I'd be pleased with a pass.'

Planning the essay

Deep: 'Obviously notes and books are important. Then there are critics in the various journals. That gives a broad outline and you can always agree with them or disagree; it gives a starting point from which to work.'

Surface: 'The lecturer tells us the basic points are in the lecture notes. Then it's a matter of matching up those with selections from one or two of the recommended critiques.'

Writing strategies

Deep: 'I do check the spelling and the grammar, but that's really no problem at all. No, it's repetition, redundancy . . . and the contradictions I have made. . . . They're my real concerns when editing.'

Surface: 'I just reread the draft, check that it's clear to read, haven't left out words, if the spelling's OK. I try to turn in the first draft, or maybe the second, so I don't want to alter too much.'

Source: Adapted from Biggs (1988) and reproduced with permission of the author and Plenum Publishing Corporation.

The data showed that, for those students who had completed the course, many had shifted their conceptions of learning. Before the course began thirty (71%) of these students held naive conceptions of learning (stages 1–3), and only twelve (29%) held sophisticated conceptions (stages 4 and 5). After the eight workshops, however, seventeen (41%) held naive conceptions and twenty-five (60%) sophisticated ones. As far as the essay marks

TABLE 5.5 Workshop titles in (and numbers attending) the course designed to improve students' conceptions of learning run by Norton and Crowley

Title of workshop	Number of students	Percentage of students
1 Psychology: higher education	233	92
2 Essays: style and structure	154	64
3 Essays: analysis and argument	115	48
4 Essays: writing the essay	149	62
5 Essays: acting on essay feedback	62	26
6 Deep and surface approaches	133	55
7 Active revision	83	34
8 Examination-taking techniques	78	32

Source: Reproduced from Norton, L. S. and Crowley, C. M. (1995) 'Can students be helped to learn how to learn?' *Higher Education*, 29: 307–28, with kind permission of the authors and Kluwer Academic Publishers.

were concerned there was little difference between the marks obtained by the students, but the exam marks of the students who held a sophisticated conception of learning at the end of the course were significantly higher ($\bar{x} = 59.9$, s.d. 11.2) than were those of the students who held a naive conception ($\bar{x} = 51.9$, s.d. 8.2).

In addition, a non-standard questionnaire measure of deep and surface learning in psychology was given to the students attending workshop 6. Scores on this scale were analysed in terms of those who had attended all the course up to that point, and those who had attended none of the workshops or only one. The results showed that students attending the course did not differ from those not attending in terms of scores on the deep items in the questionnaire, but that those who had attended scored significantly lower than their colleagues on the surface items.

Norton and Dickins (1995) describe the results obtained with a slightly revised version of this course in its second year of operation. Many of the original findings were repeated. This time there were significant differences between the marks of attendees and non-attendees on both the essay grades and the examination marks. Again, it appeared that surface learning was decreased, but that there was no improvement in deep learning. However, more surprisingly, in this second study there was little difference between the students in terms of their conceptions of learning before and after the course. Twenty-five of the thirty-eight students (66%) who wrote about their conceptions of learning had low-level conceptions at the beginning of the course, but this number only reduced to twenty (53%) in this particular study.

The finding that the course reduced surface learning but did little to promote deep learning in both years is common to a number of studies of the effects of introducing courses on approaches to study (see, e.g., the studies outlined in Gibbs, 1992). Changing teaching methods and approaches may help some students to become deeper learners, but it is clear that other institutional constraints embedded in the demand for low-cost modular systems may have more over riding considerations as far as the students are concerned. It is a sad fact that many courses today contain those features (listed on p. 51 in Chapter 3) that are likely to encourage surface learning.

Transferable skills and life-long learning

None the less, new courses on study skills, and new methods of teaching and assessment (see Chapters 6 and 7), are highlighting current concerns with the need to encourage students to become deeper learners and to develop what are termed capacities for **life-long learning** and **transferable skills**.

According to Knapper (1995), the term 'life-long learning' is used to suggest that students should leave higher education with the ability and motivation to continue learning throughout the rest of their lives, and to do this from a wide variety of sources – not just formal educational institutions. Knapper describes 'idealised' life-long learners as people with the following competencies:

- the capacity to set personal and realistic goals;
- the ability to apply existing knowledge and skills effectively;

- the ability to evaluate their own learning;
- the ability to locate information from different sources; and
- the capacity to use different learning strategies in different situations.

A more precise specification of such skills might be drawn from work on teaching 'transferable' skills. Here the argument is that students of the future, irrespective of their subject discipline, should be competent in, for example, the skills of:

- reading;
- writing;
- numeracy;
- communicating in groups;
- speaking in public;
- communicating with graphic displays; and
- using information technology.

These ideas about transferable skills and life-long learning do not just apply to students leaving university; they apply to everyone. However, recent surveys published by the Department for Education and Employment in the UK have shown that, although most young people and adults believe that learning is important, only about a third of adults in the UK have actually done any learning in the last three years, and a third have not done any since leaving school (DfEE, 1996). Clearly, the notion of life-long learning has a long way to go.

Further reading

Baxter Magolda, M. B. (1992) *Knowing and Reasoning in College: Gender-related Patterns in Student's Intellectual Development*, San Francisco, CA: Jossey Bass. A discussion of Perry-type issues, with especial reference to how there may be sex differences in what students think important about learning and studying.

Clanchy, J. and Ballard, B. (1993) *How to Write Essays: A Practical Guide for Students*, London: Longmans. Useful guide, with a good section on what tutors look for in assessing social-science essays.

Heffernan, T. M. (1997) *A Student's Guide to Studying Psychology*, Hove: Psychology Press. A specific study guide for psychology students. Guides (amongst other things) to writing essays and practical reports, taking examinations and getting the best out of lectures and tutorials.

Hettich, P. I. (1992) *Learning Skills for College and Career*, Pacific Grove, CA: Brooks/Cole. A typical study guide, which has the added advantage of relating study skills to life-long learning.

New technology and learning

I N THIS CHAPTER I first consider the uses and effectiveness of computer-aided learning and describe research on computer-aided reading and writing. I then consider computer-aided writing in the future and, in conclusion, outline some possible contributions of new technology to life-long learning.

■

Computer-aided learning (CAL)

There have always been devices to aid instruction, and the computer is but the latest in a long list. In terms of computer-aided learning it is usual to acknowledge the early ground-breaking work of Pressey in the 1920s, followed by that of Skinner, Crowder and Pask in the 1950s and 1960s. The 1970s saw the development of instruction with mainframe computers, and the 1980s and 1990s saw the introduction of micro and personal computers (PCs). Limitations of space prevent me, unfortunately, from giving more details, but Reiser (1987) and Saettler (1990) provide good accounts of the early history of computer-aided learning and of educational technology.

As Table 6.1 shows, computers – once a rarity in our schools – are now becoming commonplace. Today many students at university have their own machines and, if they do not have their own, they have access to university-wide PC labs. Today's PCs run more sophisticated programs, have colourful screens and greater amounts of storage space than ever before. Programs have become more complex, with fancy graphics, animation and in

TABLE 6.1 Figures to indicate how the numbers of microcomputers are increasing in UK schools

	Number of micros per school		
	Primary	Secondary	Special
1984–5	2	13	
1989–90	4	40	
1991–2	7	58	
1993–4	10	85	15
1995–6	13	96	19
	Number of pupils per micro		
1984–5	107	60	
1989–90	40	18	
1991–2	25	13	
1993–4	18	10	5
1995–6	15	9	4

Note: There are wide variations around these average figures.
Source: Data collated from various *Statistical Bulletins* published by the Department for Education.

some cases video and sound. In addition, electronic mail (e-mail) and the 'World-Wide Web' (WWW) allow individuals to contact other individuals and groups around the world.

It is generally argued by supporters of new technology that CAL has several advantages over conventional classroom learning. These claimed virtues are that:

● learning is individualised;
● learning is self-paced;
● there can be instant feedback upon responding;
● the programs have been written by experts, and tried and tested before being published; and
● the whole procedure can be cost-effective.

Each of these 'advantages' however, is open to discussion, if not dispute. Thus:

- there is considerable evidence for the effectiveness of paired or groupwork in CAL;
- the pacing of the learner may well be controlled by other (social) factors;
- the feedback is constrained by what is available in the program, and thus it cannot – unlike a teacher – take account of unforeseen responses;
- some programs are not well written or properly evaluated; and
- CAL is expensive.

These issues are well debated in the various textbooks and journal articles cited in this chapter.

There are many ways in which new technology has been used in our schools and colleges. Box 6.1 illustrates some of these with reference to the teaching of psychology.

The overall picture of the use of new technology in higher education is diverse. University and college environments have their own 'campus-wide networks' and facilities for word-processing, statistical analysis, information retrieval, messaging, conferencing and programming are available to students and staff. Individual departments also develop their own subject-specific facilities, which may or may not include the construction of their own programs and WWW pages for teaching purposes.

There are two developments taking place in psychology in the UK as part of the current British Government's Teaching and Learning Technology programme.

- First, there is a specific courseware development programme located at Queen's University, Belfast, which involves several disciplines other than psychology but in which psychology plays a dominant role.
- Second, there is a multi-site general courseware development project known as PsyCLE (Psychology Computer-based Learning Environment), which is co-ordinated by the CTI (Computers in Teaching Initiative) centre for Psychology at York University (http://www.york.ac.uk/inst/ctipsych).

The aim of PsyCLE is to provide an integrated software package designed to support the teaching of introductory psychology. The package is designed to be flexible and adaptable to the needs of students and lecturers, and consists of individual modules, which may be used separately or as part of the whole package. The contents include tutorial guidance, video, interactive demonstrations, simulations, experiments and problem-solving activities. Future releases will be supported by facilities designed to help the students to use the system in general. Such facilities will include tools to aid planning experiments, overviewing and navigating, taking notes, developing **concept-maps** of the material, and allowing interaction by way of conferencing. The project involves approximately thirty-six different sites, some from overseas, which fulfil either development or evaluative roles.

Despite all this activity, though, many people would argue that there has been a lack of rigorous evaluation of CAL with university students in the UK. It is generally assumed that CAL is a good thing, and that student's comments, together with those of the staff involved, are sufficient for evaluation purposes. In the USA matters are a little different, and there have been a number of attempts to evaluate more seriously the instructional effectiveness of computer-aided instruction.

Kulik *et al.* (1980) carried out a meta-analysis of fifty-nine independent evaluation studies conducted at college level in the USA. Their results indicated that for the computer-aided classes:

- the students learned more quickly;
- the students held slightly more positive attitudes towards their instruction;
- the overall effect-size was 0.25 standard deviations – which the authors regarded as 'a small effect' (see Chapter 1); and that
- the differences in examination performance were less marked with those groups that had the same teacher for the traditional or the CAL sessions.

More recently, Lipsey and Wilson (1993) summarised the results from twelve separately published meta-analyses of the effects of

BOX 6.1 Some examples of different ways of using new technology in psychology

Direct and supplementary instruction
Programs on – and demonstrations of – e.g., perceptual phenomena, statistical procedures, techniques in psychophysics . . .

Interactive tutorials
Interactive – question and answer – programs on materials taught by direct instruction by computer or by traditional methods . . .

Experiments for students to participate in as subjects
Learning tasks, signal detection studies, questionnaire/personality measures . . .

Experiment generators
Software to assist staff and/or students to prepare and run experiments . . .

Simulations
Modelling the learning of laboratory rats; comparing the effects of manipulating variables on the outcomes from statistical tests . . .

Databases
PsycLIT, Library On-line . . .

CAL. These analyses spanned the whole educational spectrum – from special school to university. Here, my calculation of the overall effect-size from Lipsey and Wilson's data shows it to be +0.36 – a modest indication of the superiority of CAL. Of course, as noted in Chapter 1, such meta-analytic reports as those by Kulik *et al.* and Lipsey and Wilson need to be read closely, for there is a wide range of findings and issues hidden under these statistical averages. And, we must not forget, students do not

BOX 6.1 *Continued*

Electronic communication
E-mail between staff and students, bulletin boards, tutorials, electronic journals, special interest groups on the WWW . . .

(Self-)Assessment
Revision exercises with multiple-choice questions – e.g., on first-year course materials . . .

Study guides
Guidance on essay writing, library skills, etc.

Non-instructional uses
Word-processing, use of spreadsheets, personality testing . . .

Examples of how psychologists use new technology can be found in articles in journals such as *The Psychologist* and *Teaching of Psychology*. *Psychology Teaching Review* devotes special issues to the topic on an occasional basis, and *Psychology Software News* provides an international forum for discussion on the use of computers in teaching psychology. Examples of the use of new technology in other disciplines can also be found in *Active Learning* and the *Association for Learning Technology (ALT) Journal*.

actually learn from the computers – they learn from the materials that the computers present. These materials can – like everything else – vary in quality and in what they require their learners to do. Finally, of course, computer technology has changed a good deal since these studies were done.

Notwithstanding the lack of rigorous evaluation studies in the UK, we all recognise that the new technology is here to stay. Accordingly, then, we need to see how best it can be used. I thus turn now from considering the effectiveness of CAL to examining how new technology can be used to aid study skills, particularly those of reading and writing.

New technology and reading

Current research on new technology and reading comes in two (overlapping) forms. First, there is a strong interest in how we can use the potential of electronic communication to enhance the presentation of books and journals. This leads us to issues of hypertext, and of **hypermedia**. Second, there is a rather more particular concern with how we can focus on particular aspects of hypertext to aid reading and studying itself.

Hypertext So what is hypertext? Figure 6.1 shows the contents page of David Jonassen's (1989) *Hypertext/Hypermedia* – a text-based illustration of hypertext. You may start to read wherever you like. However, if, for example, you turn to page 5 to study the characteristics of hypertext, you will find another circular 'hypermap'. Now you can choose to read any one of fourteen more text fragments in any order you decide. And, when reading these fragments, you can cross refer to other 'pages'. The main topics, if you like, are called *nodes* (or points of departure for several different issues) and each node and issue has connecting *links* across the text. *Hypermedia* adds video, animation, pictures and sound to hypertext.

Jonassen's hypertext was written in a text-based format simply in order to illustrate the concept. Most hypertexts are, however, computer based and the information is presented on screen. This gives them immediate advantages and disadvantages. The advantages are that (1) one can store an enormous amount of material in a much less bulky fashion, and (2) one can make connections and links almost instantaneously. The disadvantages are that (1) screen-based text is not the easiest thing in the world to read – although this is improving; (2) it is less portable; and (3) it is difficult to keep track of where you are – and where you have been – in 'hyperspace'.

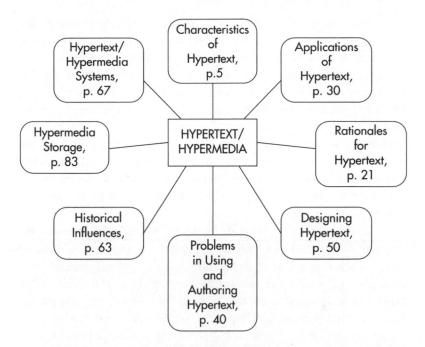

FIGURE 6.1 The 'contents page' from D. H. Jonassen's (1989) *Hypertext/Hypermedia* (reproduced with permission of the author and Educational Technology Publications)

None the less, encyclopaedias, dictionaries, handbooks and databases are particularly well suited to this approach. Electronic versions of these materials typically present materials in the traditional way, but with some additional enhancements. Thus, for example, it is far easier to search *PsycLIT* than it is to search *Psychological Abstracts* because of the former's facility for searching linked descriptors (as well as its much-reduced bulk).

Computer-aided reading and studying   Some kinds of hypertext have been developed specifically with the aim of helping readers to learn and study more effectively. For some reason, these are perhaps better known as 'electronic books'. Here I give examples of three approaches to this issue.

My first example shows how you can do things differently with an electronic text. Fox (1989), in a electronic version of a set of guidelines on how to communicate clearly, provides a set of rules for making tables in text easier to understand. In the *printed* version of these guidelines there is an illustration on a left-hand page of a poorly designed table, and an improved version of the same table on the opposite right-hand page. The printed text explains the procedures used to improve the table (such as resequencing the elements to meet the readers' requirements, respacing the columns to clarify the contents, and the introduction of line-spacing at appropriate intervals to help the readers search along the rows).

In the *hypertext* version, however, the screen presents the original table, and the reader is invited to see how the table changes when any one of these procedures is applied. Readers are thus able to see 'at the touch of a button' how the clarity of a table can be enhanced by the application of each specific guideline. In other words, the hypertext adds to this printed text by illustrating dynamically what happens when you apply guidelines for improving it, both separately and in combination.

Other examples like this within electronic books include the facility (1) to link items in footnotes, glossaries, indices and references, should the reader wish it, and (2) to 'hide' the references and items in the glossaries unless the reader asks for them by clicking on the appropriate place.

The second example of how electronic texts can aid reading involves restructuring the texts to make them more appropriate to the readers' needs. Landauer and colleagues (1993), for example, described what they call their 'SuperBook' program. In principle, any textbook can be scanned into this SuperBook program. The program creates what they term a 'rich index' (by including all of the words in the text, together with acceptable synonyms not included by the author). When readers indicate which topic they wish to study, the program will display a contents page (which is not necessarily that of the original author) that indicates where this topic occurs, and how many times it is mentioned in a particular place. Furthermore, a 'fish-eye' view of this information –

analogous to a wide-angle lens – is also available that shows the central portion of text in detail, and neighbouring areas in progressively less detail. Finally, when a topic is called up for study, this topic is presented at the top of a fresh page – so readers can easily start reading at the beginning of the page.

The SuperBook system has gone through several versions and a new, more accessible 'Mitey' book for use on PCs has been developed. Tests of this smaller version have indicated that readers can find material more quickly, and answer test questions more accurately than they can using the original printed text (Landauer *et al.*, 1993).

The third example of using hypertexts to aid study comes from the world of study skills itself. Not only are there hypertexts on study skills (e.g., see Creanor *et al.*, 1996; Tait *et al.*, 1995; Winne *et al.*, 1994) but also hypertexts which include self-study guides to particular texts (e.g., see Flora and Logan, 1996; McGlade *et al.*, 1996; Mooney *et al.*, 1995).

Portier and van Buuren (1995) describe in this context a hypertext prepared for a distance-learning course that allowed students to access the course materials in a flexible way. Students using this text were able to choose (on the basis of their prior knowledge) whether they wished to use any text-support devices such as examples, exercises, illustrations and simulations. The authors found that students learned as much from the electronic version of their text as they did from the printed one, but that students with high prior knowledge made *greater* use of the support devices in the electronic text than students with low prior knowledge. Students with low prior knowledge preferred to keep to the basics: whereas students with high prior knowledge were able to accommodate extra information more easily.

Perhaps, as an aside, we should note here that there is much exciting research work along these lines with learning-disabled readers (e.g., see Barnes and Coles, 1995; Gill, 1996; Hawkridge and Vincent, 1994; Hegarty, 1991; Roe, 1995). Visually impaired students, for example, may choose the size of print, the typeface and the format of text to suit themselves. There are computer programs that turn print into Braille, for example, and vice versa.

There are explorations with different keyboards, and with different ways of communicating with the blind, the deaf, the physically and the multiply handicapped. Developments with voice-activated programs and audio-output are also well advanced in this area of electronic communication.

These different examples show, then, how texts can be improved and reading facilitated for an enormous range of people. There is much scope for psychological research in this area. There is, for example, debate about how to write, structure and present these materials, as well as about how to evaluate them.

New technology and writing

In this section I want to discuss how new technology can help people plan, write and revise written text. In doing this, I think it helpful to think about computer-aided writing programs at three levels of complexity. These are:

- *Level 1* Simple programs used for word-processing – making deletions and substitutions, moving paragraphs and sentences about, and printing text in attractive formats.
- *Level 2* More complex programs that add to the above – e.g., style, spell and grammar checkers, and programs that assist with the preparation of indexes and references.
- *Level 3* Even more complex programs that aid writing at a higher level – programs that help with the planning and organising of the material.

Level 1 programs There has been a great deal of research on using word-processors simply to process text (see, e.g., Bangert-Drowns, 1993). The authors of studies of writing with word-processors at this level draw particular attention to:

- How much easier it is for young children to write with a keyboard than with a pen or pencil.
- How much easier it is to read printed rather than hand-written text.

- How much easier it is to make corrections (e.g., of spelling) on screen, compared with writing with pen and paper. Every version looks neat and tidy, unlike corrected hand-written text.

- How much is *lost* through this process. Some critics argue that it is hard to see or understand the processes involved in writing when crossings out, insertions, and revised sequences don't appear, and when previous versions are eliminated.

Generally speaking the authors of articles about simple word-processors at all levels of the educational system predict that word-processing will lead to more drafting, longer texts and texts of better quality. There is some evidence to support these claims, but much of this evidence is equivocal (see Chapter 5, and Bangert-Drowns, 1993; Haas, 1996). Many studies are simply not long enough, and the participants not practised enough with word-processing systems for fair comparisons to be made.

Level 2 programs More complex computer-aided writing programs aid the composition of word-processed text as well as just the word-processing of it. Spell checkers provide a limited example at this level, but grammar checkers such as *Grammatik 5* provide more sophisticated examples. Box 6.2 below lists the kinds of errors that *Grammatik 5* detects and Figure 6.2 shows a typical example of the kind of information that another package, *Grammar Checker*, provides. Programs such as these can be run after composing the text, or concurrently whilst composing it.

Recent studies of grammar checkers have focused on making comparisons between different programs to see which is the more effective at helping people to write (e.g., see Kohut and Gorman, 1995). Other studies have concentrated more on highlighting their deficiencies (e.g., see Dale and Douglas, 1996). Harris (1996) and Sydes and Hartley (1997), for instance, have demonstrated that different programs give different measures of text readability when, ostensibly, they are supposed to be using the same **read-ability formulae**. Pennington (1993) suggests that grammar checkers should not be used by second-language learners, or by

BOX 6.2 Examples of different types of error detected by *Grammatik 5* (1992)

Grammatical errors	Mechanical errors	Stylistic errors
adjective errors	spelling errors	long sentences
adverb errors	capitalisation errors	wordy sentences
article errors	double word	passive tenses
clause errors	ellipsis misuse	end of sentence
comparative/	end of sentence	prepositions
superlative use	punctuation	split infinitives
double negatives	incorrect	clichéd words/
incomplete	punctuation	phrases
sentences	number-style errors	colloquial language
noun-phrase errors	question-mark	Americanisms
object of verb	errors	archaic language
errors	quotation-mark	gender-specific
possessive misuse	misuse	words
preposition errors	similar words	jargon
pronoun errors	split words	abbreviation errors
sequence of tense		paragraph
errors		problems
subject–verb errors		questionable word
tense changes		usage

Note: One difficulty with these programs as they currently exist is that you have to have a good working knowledge of grammar to understand them – and this tends to defeat the objective.

non-proficient writers. In an earlier paper (Hartley, 1984), I suggested that authors should use both human and computer aids to editing – both have advantages and disadvantages – and this is a view that I still hold.

Level 3 programs A number of investigators are now considering how programs might be written that will aid the composing process in an even more sophisticated way. In addition to work,

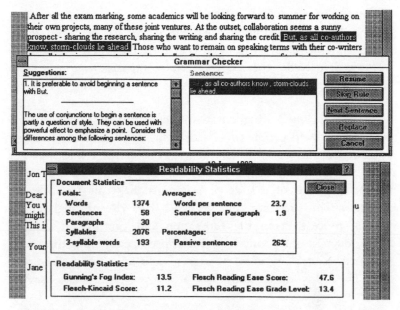

After all the exam marking, some academics will be looking forward to summer for working on their own projects, many of these joint ventures. At the outset, collaboration seems a sunny prospect - sharing the research, sharing the writing and sharing the credit But, as all co-authors know, storm-clouds lie ahead Those who want to remain on speaking terms with their co-writers

Grammar Checker

Suggestions:

1. It is preferable to avoid beginning a sentence with But.

The use of conjunctions to begin a sentence is partly a question of style. They can be used with powerful effect to emphasize a point. Consider the differences among the following sentences:

Sentence:
..., as all co-authors know , storm-clouds lie ahead

Resume
Skip Rule
Next Sentence
Replace
Cancel

Readability Statistics

Document Statistics			
Totals:		Averages:	
Words	1374	Words per sentence	23.7
Sentences	58	Sentences per Paragraph	1.9
Paragraphs	30		
Syllables	2076	Percentages:	
3-syllable words	193	Passive sentences	26%

Readability Statistics			
Gunning's Fog Index:	13.5	Flesch Reading Ease Score:	47.6
Flesch-Kincaid Score:	11.2	Flesch Reading Ease Grade Level:	13.4

FIGURE 6.2 A 'page' from the *Grammar Checker* – a computer-aided writing package

Note: *Here the writer is checking on the readabilty of her document. Note that the text the reader is working on is at the top, and there is concurrent advice being given about starting a sentence with 'But'.*

for example, on computer-generated abstracts (e.g., see Paice, 1994) and facilities for translation (e.g., see A. Hartley and Paris, 1997), researchers are now considering how programs might be written that will aid the planning and the organisational side of writing. Kellogg (1994), for instance, discusses three main difficulties that writers face in this connection:

- attentional overload – having to cope with too many processes at once;
- idea bankruptcy – a failure to generate usable ideas; and
- anxiety and emotion – which can lead to so-called 'writer's block'.

Kellogg describes a variety of computer programs that help to deal with these fundamental difficulties. 'Funnel' programs channel the writer's attention into only one or two processes at a time. 'Inventor' programs help the writer to form and relate concepts; and 'therapist' programs give feedback and reassurance to the writer. Kellogg describes several computer programs under each heading, as well as programs that combine these different functions.

In the United Kingdom work on developing sophisticated programs to help people to write is being conducted by, amongst others, Sharples and his colleagues (see Sharples and van der Geest, 1996). Sharples (1994) and Sharples *et al.* (1989) describe the development of a suite of programs they call *The Writer's Assistant*. This program aims 'to assist the writer throughout the writing process, from the generation and capture of ideas to the production of a connected piece of prose, combining the effects of a text editor, an "ideas processor" and an "outliner" editor'.

The following scenario illustrates how writers might use *The Writer's Assistant*:

> A writer wants to produce a study of 'Pottery in North Eastern Brazil' so, on entering the system, she selects the option for creating a new document. As she is writing for a newspaper colour supplement she selects Newspaper Article from a menu of options, getting a structure template and set of constraints appropriate to that type of text. The writer has a fairly firm idea of how the article will fit together, so she starts working in the structure view, sketching an outline for the body of the text by calling up the structure guide to instantiate four main sections headed 'background', 'development of pottery industry', 'evaluation' and 'conclusion' . . .
>
> With the overall structure established, our writer chooses to brainstorm ideas for the 'development of pottery industry' section. She turns to the notes network view where she sees a note for each of the sections she created in the structural view. She creates notes for subtopics, linking them to the main note with 'aspect' links. To concentrate on one subject – 'description of pottery' – she selects a presentation

of the notes network in which that note is displayed in the centre of the screen and then creates further notes to surround it . . .

The author might then switch to a linear view to find that the system has made an attempt to linearize the notes network into a list of sections and subsections, based on link types. After making some rearrangements she fills out the section headings with text for the article, moving between different perspectives of the linear view to see sections in detail or outlined, until the article is finished.

(Sharples *et al.*, 1989, p. 73)

Computer-aided writing in the future

Computer-aided writing is in a process of rapid development (see Sharples and van der Geest, 1996). So what futures might students face in this field? I envisage at least three:

- Students and staff will be more involved in interactive and collaborative work.
- There may be changes in how people think and write.
- There will be changes in how writing and learning is assessed.

Interactive and collaborative work It is now possible, using e-mail and the WWW, to send messages electronically to all parts of the world. In this broad context many computer-conferencing facilities have been set up, and many people join special interest groups to communicate electronically with each other (Sharples, 1993; Sharples and van der Geest, 1996; Smith, 1994).

In an instructional context these facilities can be copied and adapted. The discussions may be more local – involving a small group – and more focused – the tutor in charge might set specific topics and readings for discussion. (These readings, too, might be available on screen.) Tutors might ask for, and give comments on, essay plans using e-mail (e.g., see Hansen and Gladfelter, 1996). Tutors might set search tasks requiring the use of the WWW.

Velayo and Venkateswaran (1992) described the reactions to such a course by forty psychology undergraduates (twenty-three men and seventeen women) at the University of Michigan. These students had no previous experience of using computer conferencing, and were required to respond and exchange ideas using e-mail about specific issues discussed each week by the tutor. For example, one weekly discussion was about memory, and they had to respond to questions such as: 'What are some of the strategies that you use in trying to remember information when you are preparing for an exam?' 'What memory strategies presented in class do you think will be helpful in your own learning? Why so?' Each student took part in a group that used computer conferencing in addition to their normal instructional procedures.

The students' perceptions and evaluations of the course were measured by pre- and post-test questionnaires. The students rated aspects of the course using seven-point rating scales. Table 6.2 shows the mean scores on items from the questionnaire for the pre- and post-test. It can be seen that there was an improvement in the scores on most items. The students pointed out that they particularly liked computer conferencing because (1) it provided them with the opportunity to express their views in a 'less-threatening' environment, and (2) it reduced their feelings of anonymity. They also suggested several ways in which the use of computer conferencing could be improved.

Electronic networks such as these may also allow students to collaborate in the writing of essays and reports. That is, instead of individual students working on single essays independently, two or more students may send each other drafts of parts of the text that together will form a single document. Another possibility is that one student (say, in the second year) might advise another one (say, in the first year). There is considerable evidence that such 'peer-group tutoring' has positive effects on traditional student writing (Topping, 1996), so there is no reason why it should not work equally well, or better, with computer-aided writing. Just how the contribution of each student to the finished product would be assessed would no doubt have to be a matter for negotiation between the students and the tutors concerned.

TABLE 6.2 Mean pre- and post-test scores on questionnaire items measuring attitudes to computer conferencing recorded by students after experiencing computer conferencing in psychology

Questionnaire items	Mean pre-test score	Mean post-test score
Worthwhile	3.0	3.8
Valuable	2.9	3.1
Anxiety level	3.6	3.7
Helped motivation	2.7	2.8
Motivated participation	2.7	3.1
Helped understanding	2.7	2.9
Learned from others	2.8	3.3
Fun way to learn	2.5	2.9

Source: Adapted from Velayo and Venkateswaran (1992).

Writing and thinking   There is an ongoing debate in cognitive psychology about whether or not the process of writing affects thinking (Kellogg, 1994). Some people argue that people think first, and then write ('planners'). Others argue the reverse of this, saying that people write first and then see what they have put. This then leads them to make revisions ('revisers'). Others vary their procedures according to the task in hand ('mixed'). More colourful descriptions of these processes have been used. Neat planners have been described as 'Mozartians'; messy revisers as 'Beethovians'!

My attention was drawn forcefully to this issue of writing and thinking in the context of word-processing when I heard that Matthew, a 16-year-old acquaintance of mine, had been forbidden by his history teacher to use his word-processor when writing his history essays. Why? Well, the teacher insisted, Matthew would have to write in long-hand when sitting the examination. The teacher argued that the ways of thinking required for writing essays in long-hand under examination conditions were different from those required for writing essays at home with a word-processor.

Was the teacher right? What evidence is there that writing with a word-processor requires different kinds of thinking? And, if it does, should we ban students from using word-processors because they are not (currently) allowed in examination halls? I am not sure how one answers questions such as these. We certainly need to distinguish between processes and products. There are several possibilities:

● Writing with a word-processor might not involve any changes in processes or any changes in the resulting products.

● Writing with a word-processor might involve some changes in processes, but this may have no obvious effect on the resulting products.

● Writing with a word-processor might involve some changes in processes, and this may lead to some changes (hopefully improvements) in the resulting products.

It seems to me that more sophisticated computer-aided writing programs at levels 2 and 3 described above (see p. 111) may indeed alter people's writing processes. But whether or not this changes their ways of thinking is a moot point. I imagine that different kinds of writers will start to write with computer-aided writing programs in much the same way as they did before they obtained such aids. However, when they discover what these computer aids can offer, then their strategies may be modified. Currently, most computer-aided writing programs provide considerable help with the revision processes in writing, so we might expect 'planners' to spend more time revising and less time planning than they did before. Similarly, we might expect 'revisers' to spend more time planning – with the aid of outlines – than they did initially. Whether the resulting products will be different, or of a better quality, is a matter of conjecture.

This discussion, of course, is restricted to current students who are just starting to use computer-aided writing programs after many years of experience with handwriting. What the picture will be like with writers who have used computer-aided writing programs from birth, as it were, remains to be seen. One can't help but think that their ways of writing will be different from ours, especially when keyboards are displaced by voice-input devices. And, if writing is related to thinking, so their ways of thinking will be different too.

Computer-aided writing and examinations It seems somewhat of a paradox to encourage students to use word-processors and computer-aided writing programs in their studies but then fail to offer them these facilities in their examination halls. So undoubtedly this will change.

With the introduction of word-processors into examination systems one can envisage a progressive development. First, we might expect it to happen in subject areas where word-processing is taught, used or expected (e.g., in departments of computer science, communication and journalism). Initially, a choice will have to be provided: students must be allowed to decide whether or not to use specified word-processing facilities when taking their examinations if word-processing is not a regular part of the instruction.

Hall and McMurdo (1993) described the introduction of word-processors into the examinations for students at the Department of Communication and Information Studies at Queen Margaret College in Edinburgh in 1991, 1992 and 1993. A small group of first- and third-year students opted to do examinations with word-processors. The overall results, shown in Table 6.3, suggest that these volunteers did as well as their colleagues in year 1, but that they were not quite so successful in year 3. However, this is probably overstating the case, since the number of volunteers was small and they may have differed in many ways from their fellow students. (The experiment was abandoned in 1994.)

Similar results were obtained by Thompson (1996) for students learning Italian. Thompson compared the examination results of her 1994 and 1995 cohorts of students, who all used computers in an examination, with those obtained by other students in previous years who had taken similar exams without computers. (The 1994 students had complained that as all their coursework was done on computer, it was not fair to give them

TABLE 6.3 Mean examination scores of first- and third-year students using word-processors (WP) in examinations compared with those doing examinations in the traditional way (Hand). Second-year students were assessed solely on coursework.

	1990		1991		1992	
	Hand	*WP*	*Hand*	*WP*	*Hand*	*WP*
Year 1						
Average mark	56.2	58.8	51.2	49.0	51.6	50.9
No. of students	41	3	48	8	61	13
Year 3						
Average mark	59.0	59.2	53.0	50.8	53.7	47.7
No. of students	36	3	36	8	40	3

Source: Adapted from Hall and McMurdo (1993) with permission.

a traditional non-computer-based examination.) The results did not suggest any particular gains or losses for the students using the computers.

Of course, the debate about the necessity for exams at all is fuelled by research of this kind. Presumably, essay-type examinations measure a person's ability to use their knowledge and to discuss problems cogently in writing in a limited amount of time. Such a procedure seems hardly relevant these days. With the advent of interactive and collaborative work, and the use of databases to store material, supplying an answer to a question is now normally a collaborative procedure. And, of course, one does not have to sit in an examination hall to use a computer.

New technology and life-long learning

Today new technology is an essential component of everyday living – if not yet all of our learning. The developments described above will soon be commonplace and even passé. Universities, as they currently exist, will be remarkably transformed (Daniel,

1996). Indeed, some may not even exist at all as physical insti-tutions.

Although the use of new technology is still in its infancy we can already see that it could make contributions to all those aspects of teaching and learning that were outlined as important in Chapter 5. Using new technology, it has been claimed, can increase motivation, independence, collaboration, self-assessment and deeper learning.

Knapper (1988) examined how various facets of the then new technology might contribute to life-long learning. He focused his discussion around a summary table – which I have slightly modified and present here as Table 6.4. (I have added 'e-mail', the WWW and 'electronic books' to Knapper's list of major appli-cations of technology in education.) Knapper argued – in 1988 – that technology could contribute to life-long learning but that it would not necessarily do so in all respects. My additions to his table perhaps make technology contribute a little more.

Of course this idealistic picture needs to be put in perspec-tive. As noted in Chapter 5 the present situation – with increasing student numbers, declining resources and modularisation – is likely to lead more to surface approaches to learning than to deep ones. In this chapter I have tried to suggest how new technology might militate against this. But if new technology is only seen as a more cost-effective way of presenting information to a larger numbers of students then it, too, is likely to fail in this respect.

However, it would be nice to end this chapter on an upbeat note. Accordingly, let me offer a more Utopian view. Menges (1994) describes computer-aided classes of the future in terms of a number of possibilities. Each of these possibilities supports deep rather than surface learning, and each is more likely to instil in learners a positive attitude towards life-long learning. These possi-bilities are:

● a shift on the part of the teacher from 'information giving' to facilitating learning;
● a shift from whole-class instruction to individual and small-group learning;

TABLE 6.4 How aspects of computer-aided learning might contribute to the criteria for life-long learning

Criteria for life-long learning	Different aspects of new technology					
	Computer-aided instruction	Computer simulation	Computer-managed learning	Computer as a tool (e.g., word-processor)	E-mail, computer conferencing and WWW	Electronic books/hypertexts
Encourages active learning	Yes	Yes	?	Yes	Yes	Yes
Democratic – broadens access and shares responsibility for decision-making	No	?	?	Yes	Yes	?
Responds to individual differences among learners	Partly	Partly	Yes	?	?	Yes
Flexible (e.g., in terms of time and place of learning)	Yes	Yes	?	Yes	Yes	Yes
Motivating and relevant	?	Yes	?	Yes	Yes	Yes
Integrates knowledge from different fields	No	?	?	?	Yes	Yes
Collaborative (vs. competitive)	Can be	?	No	Can be	Can be	No
Avoids embarrassment to students	Yes	Yes	Yes	Yes	Yes	Yes
Encourages higher-order thinking	No?	Yes	?	Yes	Yes	Yes

Source: Adapted, with permission, from Knapper (1988).

- a shift from an emphasis on the more able student to one on the weaker ones – as whole-class instruction is reduced;
- a shift from all students learning the same thing to different students learning different things;
- a shift from passive learning to active learning;
- a shift from a competitive to a co-operative goal structure;
- a shift from thinking primarily in verbal terms to one where visual, oral and verbal thinking are equally at home;
- a shift from attempting to cover everything about a topic to sampling it;
- a shift from the teacher telling the student what is important to the individual, to the group discussing, in consultation with the teacher, how they are to decide this;
- a shift from giving marks to individual students to giving marks to groups or their work as a group;
- a shift from ranking students on their performance on the same materials to individual assessments based upon the work done by an individual;
- a shift from assessment based on exam performance to assessment based on products, progress and methods of learning;
- a shift from rewarding students for reproducing knowledge to rewarding them for demonstrating originality.

Further reading

Grundy, F. (1996) *Women and Computers*, Oxford: Intellect. A lively discussion of how computing is a male world, and what can be done about it.

Kellogg, R. T. (1994) *The Psychology of Writing*, New York: Oxford University Press. A useful review of most of the work on writing by psychologists with interesting discussions on computer-aided writing.

McKnight, C., Dillon, A. and Richardson, J. (eds) (1993) *Hypertext: A Psychological Perspective*, Hemel Hempstead: Ellis Horwood. A book written for psychologists by (mainly) psychologists that contains several interesting chapters – not least one by Tom Landauer and his colleagues on SuperBook.

Papert, S. (1993) *The Children's Machine: Rethinking School in the Age of the Computer*, Hemel Hempstead: Harvester Wheatsheaf. A fascinating glimpse into a possible future for CAL in our schools.
Schank, R. C. and Cleary, C. (1995) *Engines for Education*, Hillsdale, NJ: Erlbaum. A similar book to the one by Papert.

Useful WWW addresses

http://www.bps.org.uk
British Psychological Society

http://www.apa.org
American Psychological Association

http://www.psych.bangor.ac.uk
Bangor University home page, containing links to all psychology departments in institutes of higher education in the UK

http://www.host.cc.utexas.edu/world/lecture/psy
A list of online courses in psychology

http://www.york.ac.uk/inst/ctipsych
Computers in Psychology Teaching Initiative, University of York, UK

http://www.lafayette.edu/allanr/scip.html
Society for Computers in Psychology home page

Assessment

I N THIS CHAPTER, after briefly considering the aims of assessment, I present some criticisms of standard methods of assessment used in higher education. I then move on to discuss several less traditional methods of assessment designed to encourage deeper learning in students. I conclude with some criticisms of the research on these topics and present some final tips for students.

■

It has often been acknowledged that assessment drives what people do when they are learning and studying. Boud (1995) remarks, 'Every act of assessment gives a message to students about what they should be learning and how they should go about it.' Furthermore, he continues, 'Assessment messages are coded, not easily understood, and are often read differently and with different emphases by staff and students.' So, if we want to change what learners do, we need (1) to change our methods of assessment, and (2) to clarify our intentions.

The aims of assessment

Assessment is a multi-purpose activity – indeed, some of its different aims have conflicting purposes. Rowntree (1987) distinguishes between five different aims as follows:

● *To provide a basis for selection* In many situations there are too many applicants for the places available. Examination results, even though they have their faults, are data which can be used to assist this process.

- *To maintain standards* Giving the same examinations (or parallel versions of them) at regular intervals allows us (1) to see if the same level of performance is being achieved over time, and (2) to set similar levels for selection purposes.
- *To motivate learners* Assessment deadlines (e.g., for coursework, projects, essays) encourage learners to complete their learning by set dates.
- *To inform learners about their progress* Knowledge of results enables learners to identify their strengths and weaknesses, and to modify their subsequent behaviour accordingly.
- *To inform teachers about their progress* Course evaluations, and examination and/or test results, provide information to teachers about the effectiveness of their instruction.

Undoubtedly, we can add more aims to this list. For example, we might think that assessment controls what students do rather than motivates them to do what they would like to do.

Be that as it may, most methods of assessment lend themselves to several of these aims. Thus, for example, carrying out projects allows the learners to learn about the subject matter in question; it allows them to practise the skills of written communication; and it allows tutors to assess the learners' achievements in these respects. But the information gained will vary considerably according to whether the tutor or the student determines the topic of investigation. Rowntree (1987) has an interesting chapter on the hidden 'side-effects' of assessment.

Traditional methods of assessment

Essay examinations Rowntree (1987) comments that Britain is too essay ridden, and especially too examination-essay ridden. Indeed, it seems hard to agree that writing essays in examinations is an appropriate way to meet all the aims of assessment listed above.

Furthermore, a major difficulty with essay-examination marking is that the process itself is unreliable (and hence invalid) on at least three main counts:

- student variability on the day is not taken into account;
- independent examiners allocate different marks to the same script; and
- the same markers give different marks to the same scripts if they mark them again after an interval of time.

These characteristics of essay-examination marking have been known for a long time. Studies demonstrating them were published in the 1880s and 1910s – long before the classic study of Hartog and Rhodes (1936). And similar studies, with similar findings, have been published ever since (e.g., see Newstead, 1996).

In addition to these major sources of unreliability in examination marking there is also work which shows that the length of the essay, the quality of the handwriting, marker fatigue and the position of the script in a series (e.g., after a run of good or poor answers) can all affect the marks awarded (Marshall and Powers, 1969).

A number of ways of making essay-examination marking more reliable has been tried. Each method does not entirely solve the problem, but each is worth considering. Box 7.1 lists some possible improvements in essay-exam procedures. Research on most of these methods is discussed by Beard and Hartley (1984), Newstead (1996) or Swanson *et al.* (1997). None of these methods addresses the question, of course, of whether examination essays are a useful, or indeed the only, way of assessing learning.

Multiple-choice (or objective) tests   Multiple-choice tests are said to be more reliable than essay tests, but they, too, have their problems. And, to parallel Rowntree's (1987) remark about essay marking in Britain, we might consider assessment in the USA to be dominated by multiple-choice testing. Students in the USA, for

BOX 7.1 Some ways of improving essay examinations

Using agreed marking schemes
Implies that there are agreed answers – supports surface learning?

Writing short notes on . . .
Useful for testing factual knowledge – supports surface learning?

Increasing the number of markers
Not so viable these days . . . but certainly at least two markers should mark independently any work that contributes towards a degree classification.

Introducing 'blind marking'
Removing names from scripts is seen by some as essential. It may not reduce bias completely – people can recognise the sex of the author from most handwriting – but it should remove bias that comes from knowing the candidate.

Blind marking of word-processed scripts
Should remove bias due to sex of handwriting as well as knowledge of the author.

Open-book essay examinations
All students need to have the necessary book(s) – again not so easy these days. They also need to know the book well if they are to find information quickly.

'Seen' papers – in advance
Tends to be seen by students as a memory task – leading to surface learning.

example, complete regular multiple-choice tests in their courses, sometimes even weekly, and American 'essay' examinations often require what we in the UK would call 'short notes'.

Multiple-choice tests are quick to administer, and easy to mark. The marks are consistent between different markers (they can be machine scored), and feedback can be given quickly to the students concerned. And, because reading and answering the questions takes so little time, a large number of items can be set and all of the syllabus covered. This can lead to wide ranges of marks that differentiate well between candidates.

Some critics of multiple-choice tests claim, however, that such tests only measure factual information, and that this encourages surface/memory learning. Others think that this view is simplistic, and that it is quite possible for questions to be written that require higher-order thinking skills (e.g., see Swanson *et al.*, 1997). Whatever the case, there is some evidence that students prepare differently for different types of exams (Scouller and Prosser, 1994). Furthermore, the results may be distorted by guessing. Elaborate statistical procedures have been developed to counteract this.

Good multiple-choice test questions take time to develop, but 'banks' of such questions are available. Such tests may prove useful in studies of the effectiveness of different courses taught in different institutions, for the same tests can be given to different groups. Thus there may be some value in using them in Britain (as in the USA) as part of any attempt to measure an agreed national curriculum in a subject such as psychology (Howarth and Croudace, 1995).

Coursework Today the final marks for modules are usually made up from a number of sources. These typically include marks from essays and from coursework, and sometimes marks from other components, such as student presentations, are also included. There is considerable variation between and within institutions about the relative weightings given to these different components. Coursework, of course, has several advantages over end-of-semester examinations. It is less concentrated, avoids poor performance on a 'bad day', and removes the fear of unanticipated questions. Thus students think it 'fairer' (Kniveton, 1996). Furthermore, coursework is often more authentic and closer to real life than is that done sitting an examination. Coursework, therefore, is more likely to encourage deeper learning.

There, are of course, disadvantages. Students can select what they are going to work on – they do not have to cover the full syllabus. Opportunities for cheating and plagiarism are higher (Diekhoff *et al.*, 1996; Newstead *et al.*, 1996). The work takes longer to mark and to check. And, of course, the concerns about the reliability of marking discussed above in connection with essay marking still remain.

When discussing the pros and cons of coursework assessment differences between students are sometimes considered. It is often said, for example, that mature students are more likely to appreciate a form of assessment that allows them to study in depth but, as we have seen from Chapter 4, this consideration is likely to apply to most students. None the less, some students might prefer to be assessed by examinations and to avoid what they see as the relentless stress of coursework.

Studies of coursework assessment generally show that students do in fact gain higher marks on coursework components than they do on examinations. Accordingly, some departments weight these components differently in order to overcome this. However, as Alan Branthwaite and I showed some years ago, by using computer simulations, the effects of minor changes in the weightings of different components has little effect on the final outcome. Indeed, we found that both staff and students over-estimated the importance of slight changes in marks in determining the final results (Hartley and Branthwaite, 1977).

Projects and dissertations   There has been little work done on the reliability and validity of assessing project work in psychology – or, indeed, in other subject matters (Henry, 1994). Many of the objections to the marking of essays also apply to the marking of projects. Projects are normally marked by the supervisor and one other person, so the supervisor cannot mark 'blind', even if the project is handed in for marking without the author's name (Dennis *et al.*, 1996). Decisions have to be made about the amount of work done by the student, the contribution of the supervisor to the idea, and the amount of help given with the statistics, and so on. Henry (1994) discusses some variations on these themes.

Bradley (1984) published an interesting paper that suggested that there was sex-bias present in the marking of psychology projects. In particular, she claimed to show that more-able men received higher project marks than more-able women, and that less-able men received lower project marks than less-able women. This resulted in a distribution for project marks rather like that shown in Table 3.2 (p. 38). Bradley's results attracted much attention and debate, but they do not appear to have been replicated (see Dennis and Newstead, 1994; Dennis *et al.*, 1996; Warren, 1997).

Whatever the truth of the matter, it is usually considered that a project or dissertation allows the student greater scope for learning in a deeper manner (see Cuthbert, 1995; Henry, 1994). Box 7.2 lists some responses of students on being questioned about dissertations that demonstrate this. One particular problem here, however, is than many students are unsure about what doing a project or dissertation involves (Hampson, 1994). There is certainly scope for greater clarity here, and for encouraging students to work in pairs or small groups on projects or dissertations than is the current practice (e.g., see Arnold *et al.*, 1994; Garvin *et al.*, 1995).

Variations on traditional themes

In this section I shall describe some newer methods of assessment, particularly those that are said to encourage motivation and deeper learning, and thus encourage life-long learning. Many of these methods, of course, are used in combination with traditional ones, so they do not replace them. The problem, then, is one of teasing out what are the additional advantages of a particular method of assessment, and whether or not they have occurred. As we shall see, however, in evaluating these newer methods most investigators have not utilised sophisticated methods. Most have been content to rely on questionnaire measures of opinion from staff and students, and possibly some interviews. There have been very few comparison studies.

BOX 7.2 Responses of students to what they thought a dissertation was – after they had completed it

What is a dissertation?

- It's a long drawn-out essay, usually with a conclusion at the end, but it is also a labour of love, doing research into something you are interested in.

- It's not just a long essay. It takes many weeks or months of work, both researching and writing. It includes areas not in essays such as literature reviews. When complete it looks much like, in structure and style, a book.

- To me a dissertation is lots of hard work. I'd say it's about choosing a topic you're interested in, doing lots of reading and in my case also empirical work, and then doing lots of writing in a very complicated academic style.

- It has been a process of self-discovery as well as a discovery of other things, people, ideas. It is a learning process which, although painful at some stages, 'pays off in the end'.

- It's not just academic learning and knowledge – it's everything! It's not only what you learn from the academic point of view. It's also about using computers, not being isolated, learning to work with other people – it's everything together.

Source: Responses from Hampson (1994) reproduced with permission.

Self-assessment Undoubtedly, one of the major contenders for methods of assessment that are said to contribute to deeper learning is 'self-assessment'. Self-assessment can be defined as, 'the involvement of students in identifying standards and/or criteria to apply to their own work and making judgements about the extent to which they have met these criteria and standards' (Boud, 1995).

Boud continues, 'self assessment thus means more than students grading their own work; it means involving them in the process of determining what is good work in any situation. It requires them to consider what are the characteristics of, say, a good essay or practical report and to apply this to their own work.'

Boud thus sees self-assessment as being about students' developing their own learning skills. He says that self-assessment is not just an assessment technique to be put alongside others. 'It is not about students awarding themselves grades (although this comes into it). It is about engaging learners with criteria for good practice in any given area and making complex judgements.'

Brew (1995) lists over fifty studies that examined self-assessment in twenty-one different subject matters, including, for psychology, that of an early American study by Moreland *et al.* (1981). Similarly, Boud and Falchikov (1995) review much the same literature. Boud and Falchikov point to numerous limitations in the studies covered (e.g., the use of unattributed scales of measurement; the insufficient descriptions of the context of the studies; and the general lack of clarity as to whether the self-assessments were actually used for deciding overall marks or not). However, despite these difficulties, they draw the following general conclusions:

- In most studies, the majority of the students' marks or assessments agreed with those given by the teacher. In other words, most students did not over-rate (or under-rate) their performance – although there were some studies showing over-rating and under-rating.
- By and large, high-achieving students tended to underestimate their performance, whilst low-achieving students tended to over-estimate it.
- More experienced students (say, third-year ones) tended to be better at estimating their performance relative to less experienced (first-year) ones.
- There was insufficient evidence to tell whether or not the students improved the accuracy of their ratings with practice.

- In five out of seven studies where the students' assessments contributed towards the actual grades awarded there was a tendency for the students involved to over-rate themselves.
- There were no clear sex differences in the results of six studies which looked for them.

Peer Assessment   Peer assessment is defined in the same way as self-assessment, except that peer assessment is characterised by students rating *other students* as well as themselves. (Boud [1995] actually sees this as a false distinction, since, he claims, 'one of the greatest misconceptions about self assessment is that it can be undertaken in isolation from others'.) Many studies combine self- and peer assessment together (as does that of Moreland *et al.* [1981] mentioned above).

As we saw in Chapters 2 and 6, much self- and peer assessment is built into self-paced PSI or Keller plan courses, and into computer-aided learning. In PSI courses student 'proctors' assess other students' work. Such 'peer tutoring' is generally acknowledged to be helpful – both for the peer and for the tutor (Houston and Lazenbatt, 1996; Topping, 1996).

Falchikov (1995a) described a small-scale study of peer assessment in developmental psychology. Thirteen students took part. The students were asked to go to the library, find the section with journals on developmental psychology, and to find an article that interested them on pre-adolescent psychology. They were then required to summarise the article in not more than two sides of A4, and to suggest what investigation the experimenter might do next. Finally, they were asked to prepare a ten-minute presentation for the other students.

Each of the students was asked to rate the presentations of the other twelve students – following guidelines agreed with the tutor. It was also agreed that the mean marks given by the students should carry equal weight with the marks awarded by the tutor in terms of the coursework grade. The results showed that the distribution of the marks given by the students for each student was not significantly different from that given by the tutor. Similar findings have been found in other studies of peer assessment of student presentations in other disciplines (e.g., see Freeman, 1995).

Peer assessment can be used with other types of academic work as well as presentations. It can be used for essays, project reports, examination answers and so on. However, there is debate, as with self-assessment, about whether or not the marks given by peers should be advisory for the students concerned, or should actually count in assessment situations. Both Boud (1995) and Falchikov (1995b) argue that it is better for such feedback to be advisory. Peer feedback which is used to determine final grades can, according to Boud, lead to jealousies and resentments.

Presentations   In Falchikov's (1995a) study, described above, the students were rated on their presentations of their research. Falchikov describes how the students worked out with their tutor a set of criteria between them for what they thought a good presentation should be like. They decided that such presentations should:

● have a coherent and logical structure;
● demonstrate a good knowledge and understanding of the topic;
● should include an appropriate amount of information – not too much, not too little; and
● should be delivered in a clear, expressive manner.

Presentations are becoming increasingly common these days. The technique is seen to be useful because it concentrates on spoken rather than written communication skills, and, in addition, draws attention to the presentation of tabular and graphical materials via overhead transparencies. Anholt (1994) and Kirkman (1994) give useful advice on how to give effective presentations.

Most published evaluations of presentations as a technique for learning use questionnaire studies of student (and staff) opinion (e.g., see Colman, 1996; Smit and van der Molen, 1996). However, the marks awarded for presentations are often added into other assessments. The contribution of these marks to the overall grade is usually small, but there are three difficulties to consider here. First, the criteria for what are good presentations may be vague. Second, presentations – unless they are videoed –

cannot be repeated, or remarked. Third, marks cannot be awarded 'blind'. These last two difficulties can be overcome, though, with poster papers.

Poster papers   Poster papers have been used in the teaching of psychology for some time (e.g., see Baird, 1991; Rosenberg and Blount, 1988). Berry and Houston (1995) suggest that poster sessions:

- are an excellent alternative medium for developing communication skills;
- encourage students to investigate a topic thoroughly;
- provide an opportunity for peer learning and peer assessment; and
- promote a positive attitude in students.

Furthermore, they conclude that the process of creating and speaking to posters encourages conceptual development by:

- exposing and confronting misconceptions; and
- putting the emphasis on concepts in addition to procedures.

Preparing posters is an unusual task for students – it involves group work, selection of key points from the literature, and skills in the techniques of visual presentation. Posters may be used instead of seminar presentations and presented and discussed with fellow students and staff. In this way preparing posters represents an authentic task in that it mimics the requirements of professionals.

Poster papers have been used in a variety of disciplines apart from psychology. Berry and Houston (1995) report studies in mathematics, nurse education, sociology, biology and chemistry. Hay and Miller (1992) describe how students in geography emulated professional practice by working through all the stages of research leading up to the presentation and delivery of results in a poster paper.

Learning contracts   Another example of new ways of working with students that is said to encourage deeper learning is that of the 'learning contract'. Anderson *et al.* (1996) define a learning contract as 'essentially an agreement negotiated between a learner and a staff supervisor to ensure that certain activities will be undertaken in order to achieve a learning goal and that specific evidence will be produced to demonstrate that the goal has been reached. In return, formal recognition (typically in the form of academic credit) is given for the work produced.'

Learning contracts typically list the intended aims, and the methods to be used in achieving these by a certain date. The contract is signed by both the student and the tutor. Contracts can be renegotiated should the student wish to change direction, or take more time. Such contracts, according to Anderson *et al.*, 'encourage students to accept greater responsibility for their own learning, to manage the learning process and to use their own personal experience as a basis for new learning'. Contracts mean that class-assignments can be tailored to individual learners.

There seem to be few reports of the use of learner contracts in psychology. However, Knowles (1986) does give two examples from the University of Nebraska. Each contract followed the same format – the students concerned wrote lists of related statements under the three headings of (1) Goals – where am I going? (2) How shall I get there? and (3) How will I know I've arrived? Knowles also cites some early evaluation studies of learner contracts conducted in the 1970s and 1980s and concludes that 'contract learning has been shown to be an effective mode of education in a wide variety of situations'.

Harris (1995) notes that most of the work completed under learning contracts is assessed by the staff rather than by the learner, or conjointly. This, she feels, is a device that staff use, perhaps unconsciously, to keep control of what is being done. Harris points to the value of negotiating both the methods of assessment as well as what is to be done.

Records of Achievement Records of Achievement are ways of presenting more information to people about a student's performance than is usual with, say, a single classification – for example, an upper-second-class mark. Marks for different sub-skills may be awarded. Starr (1993), for example, describes how students on one psychology course were rated on the following skills:

- communication;
- interviewing;
- behavioural experiments;
- measuring people's opinions and behaviour;
- time- and task-management;
- analysing the components of tasks;
- computing;
- group work;
- teaching; and
- statistics.

In some Records of Achievement, scores on individual skills are presented alongside the class averages. This means that not only can employers, for example, see how a student performs on each of the skills, but they can also see how that performance relates to that achieved by the rest of the class. Potterton and Parsons (1995) claim that students who know that Records of Achievement are to be provided at the end of the course change their behaviour and work harder.

Portfolios It is a small step from Records of Achievement to *portfolios*. Portfolios used to be thought of as a collection of examples of pieces of work done throughout a course to illustrate what had been achieved. Today this definition has expanded slightly in different ways. It is now conventional to include the students' reflections on their methods and achievements in putting together their portfolio and portfolios can be used for different purposes.

Finlay *et al.* (1994), for example, described how they were studying the effects of using portfolios with two groups of medical students working with cancer patients. One group was compiling a portfolio to record events, interactions, relevant articles, etc., based around the patients' case histories, whereas the other group was not doing so. Otherwise the instruction was the same. The effectiveness of the portfolios was to be indirectly assessed in clinical competence exams and by hidden questions in standard multiple-choice examinations. The aim of the study was to see whether or not the portfolios helped the students gain a better personal and technical knowledge of cancer, and whether or not the students gained greater insight into the impact of the disease and its treatment on patients and their families. Regrettably, no results have been reported (at the time of writing).

Student journals (diaries) The use of journals by students in which to record their activities, thoughts, questions, understanding, etc., is quite widespread in some areas of instruction. These journals are sometimes graded, and the grade incorporated into a final module mark, but this is quite rare. Most journals are for private consumption, although they may be handed in for tutors to read and comment on if the student so desires, or if it is made clear from the start that this is to be expected. Journals are not unlike diaries, although it is not expected that there should be a daily entry.

Probably the best-known work on journal writing in psychology is that by Hettich (e.g., Hettich, 1976 and 1990). In Hettich's (1976) study students were asked to write at least two entries per week in a notebook and to try to relate what they were learning in class and reading about to their everyday experiences. A typical entry might read thus (p. 60):

> There is a small boy around school. One day he called me 'Lulu'. I was very surprised because I do not know him. Later I learned that there is another Chinese girl around school by that name and he knew her. So, whenever he sees other Chinese girls, he calls them 'Lulu'. I think this would be an example of *stimulus generalisation*. This little boy has associated the name 'Lulu' with certain looks and features of a Chinese girl and he tends to generalise to all Chinese girls.'

In a questionnaire evaluation of this study students regarded the journal as:

- a valid measure of learning;
- a means of stimulating critical thinking;
- a source of feedback; and
- a useful supplement to examinations;

but not as a strong source of motivation for learning course materials. Some 95% of 102 respondents said that they would prefer to keep a journal than to have to write a term paper. Hettich's (1990) article describes how he has used these techniques in eleven different areas of psychology. He concluded that possibly up to 25% of a module grade could be devoted to journal entries.

McCrindle and Christensen (1995) conducted probably one of the most thorough analyses of the value of journal writing with a first-year biology course. Here forty students were randomly assigned into two groups – those keeping learning journals and those writing weekly lab reports. After five weeks, the students were assessed on (1) a Marton and Saljo-like task, (2) a learning-strategies questionnaire, and (3) a final examination. (The Marton and Saljo-like task required students to read a passage, remember the content, and then explain how they had gone about doing so: see p. 47 in Chapter 3.) The journal group displayed more sophisticated conceptions of learning on this task than the report group, and they performed significantly better than the report group on the final exam (mean score of 29.4 compared with 25.3). However, the two groups did not differ on the learning-strategies questionnaire.

Structured diaries   Fazey (1993) and Fazey and Linford (1996) described the use of a more structured or 'personal development' diary in a pilot study with a group of seven students at Bangor University studying sport, health and physical education. Here the aim was to help the students develop their skills of self-assessment. Each student was required to assess their existing competence on a range of learning skills, and to prioritise which skills they wished to develop in the next three weeks. This procedure was then repeated for the remainder of the term. Forms were provided so that the students could record their weekly practice and success on different skills, and their own assessment and that of colleagues on how well they were doing. Following this initial research a larger group activity was then developed with all the students in the class. A list of skills was provided (see Box 7.3) and students worked in groups of four or five to set targets for their group to achieve in the following three weeks as before. (Regrettably, Fazey does not report evaluation data in these publications.)

BOX 7.3 List of skills which students working in groups had to acquire in the study by Fazey

Below are some of the skills which you will be expected to acquire and use this year. An * denotes a skill which you will need to use in the next three weeks. You should, in your group, choose no more than about three other skills from each section. You should aim to practise these so that each member of the group is proficient at them within three weeks.

Word processing
using HELP
formatting disks
saving and retrieving documents on your disk
printing documents
   draft
   final form
typing in (practice of the skill)
editing
   underlining
   bold characters
   centring text
   deleting text
   moving text
   adjusting margins
   double spacing
spell-checking
copying files
* typing a reference in the prescribed format

BOX 7.3 *Continued*

Library skills
using the SSCI/BIDS to find information about:
   a subject
   an author's publications
   who has cited a particular publication
using the library catalogue to:
   search for publications by an author
   find out if a book or journal is in the catalogue
   find out if a book is on the shelves
   find out where a book is shelved
understand the Library of Congress classification
be able to photocopy information in the library
use the CD ROM system for information retrieval
* correctly complete the library-skills exercise

Writing skills
be able to research and plan an essay
describe an appropriate structure for an essay
appropriately structure paragraphs
take comprehensible notes in a lecture
précis passages from papers and books
* know how to use quotes in an essay
* use the prescribed referencing format

Reading skills
use a strategy for selecting important information in a
   text
proofreading
speed reading
use a strategy to test for your understanding in reading
identify a good place and time for reading
organise time for reading each week
* be able to read and then summarise in your own words

Source: List reproduced with permission from Fazey (1993).

Some remarks on the above studies

This chapter has described a number of different methods of assessment. I have tried to show that each has advantages and disadvantages, and that a number of evaluation studies have been carried out to assess the evidence for the various claims made by their various protagonists.

However, some rather obvious criticisms can be made here. Most investigators have focused on one particular method of assessment, and few have sought to compare different methods. Furthermore, even fewer have sought to examine how different methods of assessment might suit different kinds of individuals. Some students – as noted in Chapter 2 – may actively dislike methods of teaching and learning designed to encourage independent learning. In particular, part-time students (McDowell, 1993) and students from different cultures (Purdie and Hattie, 1997) may have different expectations and desires. And – as noted in Chapters 3 and 5 – even typical students are likely to have different preferences for methods of assessment related to their conceptions of teaching and learning (Birenbaum, 1997).

The main criticism that I want to make here, however, is a methodological one. In this chapter we have seen that quantitative methods have been used to evaluate the traditional methods of assessment, and that qualitative ones – in the main – have been used to evaluate the newer methods. Indeed, the perceptive reader will have observed that in the second part of this chapter I have not been able to report more than one or two quantitative studies that have assessed the effects of a particular method of assessment on the resulting grades or examination marks. Opinions have been sought in large measure, and generally they have been favourable. But, basically speaking, my criticism is that little hard evidence has been gathered to suggest that these new methods have any effects on 'the bottom line' – actual examination performance.

I suppose one could argue that recent research has concentrated on learning *processes* rather than learning *outcomes*, and that some processes might be better than others. But one would expect that these processes would have effects on outcomes too.

The lack of evidence – for or against this – is disappointing from a psychological perspective, particularly when there is evidence from qualitative studies that people often distort their recall of the past to make it congruent with their current beliefs (Conway and Ross, 1984).

Some concluding tips for learners

Finally, on quite a different tack, I would like to recommend some specific actions that learners might take to improve their learning and studying. It seems to me that there is no need for learners to sit around and wait for their colleagues and tutors to set up new procedures – although it might be useful to encourage them to do so. Most of the newer methods of assessment described above can be carried out without waiting for a formal structure to be created. If every learner were:

- to find a fellow learner and mutually assess their performance in aspects of their learning, such as:
  critical reading of research reports;
  lecture preparation;
  tutorial involvement;
  essay/report writing;
  exam preparation and performance; and
- to keep a reflective diary, making an entry at least once a week,

then I believe they would find themselves to be more effective learners. But that is my belief. Perhaps my readers would like to provide experiential evidence for it!

Further reading

Boud, D. (ed.) (1988) *Developing Student Autonomy in Learning* (2nd edition), London: Kogan Page.

Boud, D. (ed.) (1995) *Enhancing Learning Through Self-assessment* (2nd edition), London: Kogan Page.

Boud, D. and Feletti, G. (eds) (1997) *The Challenge of Problem Based Learning* (2nd edition), London: Kogan Page.

These three books edited by David Boud follow much the same format – an editorial introduction, some wide-ranging chapters, and then numerous case histories from different subject disciplines. The editorial chapters are very helpful.

Rowntree, D. (1987) *Assessing Students: How Shall We Know Them?* (2nd edition), London: Kogan Page. This book gives a very readable account of the problems faced by traditional and newer methods of assessment.

Glossary

The first occurrence of each of these terms is highlighted in **bold** type in the main text.

'Access' students   Students who enter higher education in the UK with few or no traditional-entry qualifications after they have successfully completed especially devised one- or two-year 'Access' courses.

advance-organisers   Devices like summaries and overviews but differ in that they provide a conceptual framework that helps readers to understand the material ahead.

analysis of variance   A statistical technique that allows you to look for main effects and interactions between variables when considering the mean scores of different groups.

archival methods   Data collected from past records (e.g., degree results in an institution for the past twenty years) and then analysed.

behaviour modification   Attempts to change behaviour based upon behavioural principles.

behavioural instruction   *See* Keller plan.

behavioural psychology A school of psychology founded on the belief that all data must come from observable behaviour, with a strong emphasis on **reinforcement**.

case histories The intensive study of one particular person or small group of persons, possibly during a particular event.

central tendency The central value of a set of scores – for example, the mean (the arithmetic average), the median (the mid-point) and the mode (the most frequently occurring score).

cluster analysis A statistical technique that divides people up into groups or 'clusters' in which every member of one cluster is more like members of that cluster than like anyone else in other clusters.

cognitive psychology A school of psychology that emphasises the role of cognition in human behaviour. **Cognition** encompasses thinking, perception, learning, memory and consciousness.

cognitive styles Ways in which different individuals characteristically approach different cognitive tasks.

computer-assisted learning Learning that is undertaken with the aid of a computer program. The instruction so provided is called **computer-assisted instruction**. Different learning experiences may be planned and executed in a **computer-managed learning** situation.

concept maps Diagrammatic representations of the main concepts of a particular topic, designed to show its structure.

conceptions of learning What learners (and teachers) believe about what learning involves.

conceptions of teaching What learners (and teachers) believe about what effective teaching involves.

constructivism A theoretical position that suggests that there is no such thing as objective reality. Everything is derived from a person's constructs or beliefs.

convergent thinking Thinking that focuses down to one correct right answer. *See also* **divergent thinking**.

crystallised intelligence Intelligence that is relatively fixed and habitual, and concerned with storing and using facts.

deep learning In contrast to **surface** learning that concentrates on remembering, **deep** learning focuses on understanding meaning.

de-schooling movement A movement in the 1960s that suggested that formal schooling should be abolished.

divergent thinking Thinking that leads to multiple – divergent – responses.

experimental methods Methods that allow for the formation of groups, especially where membership can be randomly allocated, and where one group forms the control group against which the performance of the other experimental group(s) following some treatment can be compared.

field dependence/independence Students who are said to be field dependent are closely controlled by factors in the environment (the 'field'). Hence, for example, they might be more likely to be tied to the structure and language of a text. Students who are said to be field independent are not tied so closely to such factors: they would be more likely to reorganise the text's meaning to suit their own needs and conceptions.

fluid intelligence Intelligence that allows people to solve problems, and to process information creatively.

hidden curriculum Although not directly taught this, children at school learn how to behave, what is socially acceptable, and how to hide that which is not.

hypertext Text (which is usually computer-based and presented in small sections) that allows the readers to pursue almost any sequence that they wish. **Hypermedia** incorporates video and sound into hypertext.

intelligence The ability to learn from experience, to think in abstract terms, and to deal with one's environment.

intelligence tests Tests designed to measure intelligence that have been appropriately standardised and evaluated.

Keller plan A method of teaching where students instruct themselves on topic units. Each unit has to be mastered before progress is allowed to the next one. Students are typically tested by more senior students. Also known as **PSI** (personalised system of instruction) and 'behavioural instruction'.

learning strategies Strategies that students adopt when studying. Different strategies can be selected by learners to deal with different tasks.

learning styles Ways in which individuals characteristically approach different learning tasks. Learning styles might be more automatic than **learning strategies**, which are more optional.

life-long learning Learning does not just stop after school or university. It is argued that school and university students should be taught the necessary skills to enable them to continue learning effectively throughout their lives.

locus of control   People who believe that they are in control of their own destinies are said to have a different 'locus of control' from people who believe that their lives are ruled by chance, luck and fate.

mature students   Students who are over twenty years of age on entry to higher education and who do not, therefore, come straight from school.

mean   The arithmetic average of all the scores in a distribution.

meta-analysis   A statistical technique used both to summarise the results obtained from many different studies of the same thing, and to compare sub-groups of studies within the overall sample. This is done by calculating a summary statistic – called an 'effect-size' (see p. 6).

multiple-regression   A statistical technique that allows you to make predictions about performance on one variable based on the performance on two or more other variables.

operant conditioning   A type of conditioning where an activity that is rewarded or reinforced is likely to increase, and one that is punished or not rewarded is likely to decrease.

peer assessment   Assessment by fellow students.

peer tutoring   Teaching by fellow students.

phenomenological psychology   A school of psychology that emphasises the importance of subjective experience.

problem-based learning   Problem-based courses start with problems which students attempt to solve rather than with direct instruction from a tutor.

programmed learning   A precursor of computer-based learning, where learners progressed through small stages, making responses and receiving immediate knowledge of results.

PSI   Personalised system of instruction. *See also* **Keller plan**.

qualitative methods   Methods – like case histories (see above) and interviews – which focus on description rather than numbers.

quantitative methods   Methods – like questionnaires and experiments – that provide numerical data for analysis.

readability formulae   Formulae applied to texts in order to predict their suitability for readers of different ages.

reinforcement   A consequence that increases the likelihood of the behaviour that preceded it the next time the situation occurs. **Reinforcers** also have the same effect.

rote learning   Learning by heart/parrot fashion.

standard deviation A measure of the spread of scores around a mean. If the data are normally distributed, 66% of the scores fall within one standard deviation, and 98% within two standard deviations on either side of the mean.

statistical significance If the difference between the mean scores of different groups is greater than might be expected by chance this is said to be statistically significant.

survey methods Opinions from a sample of a proportion of the population concerned are collected in order to obtain information representative of the sample as a whole.

token economy A system of behaviour modification where tokens, awarded for desirable behaviours, can be accumulated and exchanged for reinforcers of different values.

traditional-entry students Students aged 18–20 who come directly into higher education from school.

transferable skills Skills that 'transfer' to (i.e., can be applied) in many different situations (e.g., the skills of literacy and numeracy).

validity The more a measure represents what it is supposed to be measuring, then the greater is its validity.

References

Abouserie, R. (1995) 'Self-esteem and achievement motivation as determinants of students' approaches to studying', *Studies in Higher Education*, 20, 1: 19–26.

Anderson, G., Boud, D. and Sampson, J. (1996) *Learning Contracts: A Practical Guide*, London: Kogan Page.

Anderson, T. II. and Armbruster, B. B. (1991) 'The value of taking notes during lectures', in R. F. Flippo and D. C. Caverly (eds) *Teaching Reading and Study Strategies at the College Level*, Newark, DE: International Reading Association.

Anholt, R. R. H. (1994) *Dazzle 'Em with Style: The Art of Oral Scientific Presentation*, New York: Freeman.

Archer, J. (1996) 'Sex differences in social behaviour: are the social role and evolutionary explanations compatible?', *American Psychologist*, 51, 9: 909–17.

Arksey, H., Marchant, I. and Simmill, C. (eds) (1994) *Juggling for a Degree: Mature Students' Experience of University Life*, Lancaster University: Unit for Innovation in Higher Education.

Arnold, P., O'Donnell, C. and Meudell, P. (1994) 'A practical experiment', *New Academic*, 3, 2: 4–6.

Baillie, A., Porter, N. and Corrie, S. (1996) 'Encouraging a deep approach to the undergraduate psychology curriculum: an example and some lessons from a third-year course', *Psychology Teaching Review*, 5, 1: 14–24.

Baird, B. N. (1991) 'In-class poster sessions', *Teaching of Psychology*, 18, 1: 27–9.

Bangert-Drowns, R. L. (1993) 'The word-processor as an instructional tool: a meta-analysis of word processing in writing instruction', *Review of Educational Research*, 63, 1: 69–93.

Barnes, D. and Coles, C. (1995) *IT for All*, London: David Fulton.

Baxter Magolda, M. B. (1992) *Knowing and Reasoning in College: Gender-related Patterns in Students' Intellectual Development*, San Francisco, CA: Jossey Bass.

Beard, R. and Hartley, J. (1984) *Teaching and Learning in Higher Education* (4th edition), London: Paul Chapman.

Bennett, N. (1976) *Teaching Styles and Pupil Progress*, London: Open Books.

Berry, J. and Houston, K. (1995) 'Students using posters as a means of communication and assessment', *Educational Studies in Mathematics*, 29, 1: 21–7.

Biggs, J. (1988) 'Approaches to learning and to essay writing', in R. R. Schmeck (ed.) *Learning Strategies and Learning Styles*, New York: Plenum.

Biggs, J. (1996) 'Enhancing teaching through constructive alignment', *Higher Education*, 32: 347–64.

Birenbaum, M. (1997) 'Assessment preferences and their relationship to learning', *Higher Education*, 33: 71–84.

Bond, J., Coleman, P. and Peace, S. M. (eds) (1993) *Ageing in Society: An Introduction to Social Gerontology* (2nd edition), London: Sage.

Bostrom, R. N. (1990) *Listening Behavior: Measurement and Application*, New York: Guilford Press.

Boud, D. (ed.) (1988) *Developing Student Autonomy in Learning* (2nd edition), London: Kogan Page.

Boud, D. (ed.) (1995) *Enhancing Learning Through Self-assessment* (2nd edition), London: Kogan Page.

Boud, D. and Falchikov, N. (1995) 'What does research tell us about self assessment?' in D. Boud (ed.) *Enhancing Learning Through Self-assessment* (2nd edition), London: Kogan Page.

Boud, D. and Feletti, G. (eds) (1997) *The Challenge of Problem Based Learning* (2nd edition), London: Kogan Page.

Bourner, T. and Race, P. (1990) *How to Win as a Part-time Student*, London: Kogan Page.

Bradley, C. (1984) 'Sex bias in the evaluation of students', *British Journal of Social Psychology*, 23: 147–53.

Branthwaite, A., Trueman, M. and Hartley, J. (1980) 'Writing essays: the actions and strategies of students', in J. Hartley (ed.) *The Psychology of Written Communication: Selected Readings*, London: Kogan Page.

Brew, A. (1995) 'Self assessment in different domains', in D. Boud (ed.) *Enhancing learning Through Self-assessment* (2nd edition), London: Kogan Page.

Brook, I., Hunt, J. and Hughes, P. (1994) 'Constraints on student-centred learning practices', in G. Gibbs (ed.) *Improving Student Learning: Theory and Practice*, Oxford: Oxford Centre for Staff Development, Oxford Brookes University.

Brooks, C. I. and Rebeta, J. L. (1991) 'College classroom ecology: the relation of sex to classroom performance and seating preference', *Environment and Behavior*, 23, 3: 305–13.

Burda, J. M. and Brooks, C. I. (1996) 'College classroom seating position and changes in achievement motivation over a semester', *Psychological Reports*, 78: 331–6.

Capizzi, E. (1996) 'Measuring the effectiveness of Access: methods and minefields', *Journal of Access Studies*, 11, 1: 34–58.

Caverly, D. C. and Orlando, V. P. (1991) 'Textbook study strategies', in R. F. Flippo and D. C. Caverly (eds) *Teaching Reading and Study Strategies at the College Level*, Newark, DE: International Reading Association.

Chalmers, D. and Fuller, R. (1996) *Teaching for Learning at University*, London: Kogan Page.

Chen, C. and Rada, R. (1996) 'Interacting with hypertext: a meta-analysis of experimental studies', *Human–Computer Interaction*, 11, 2: 125–56.

Clanchy, J. and Ballard, B. (1993) *How to Write Essays: A Practical Guide for Students*, London: Longmans.

Clarke, S. (1988) 'Another look at the degree results of men and women', *Studies in Higher Education*, 13, 3: 315–31.

REFERENCES

Clennell, S. (ed.) (1984) 'Older students in the Open University', report from the Older Students' Research Group, Open University, Milton Keynes.

Cohen, G., Stanhope, N. and Conway, M. (1992) 'Age differences in the retention of knowledge by young and elderly students', *British Journal of Developmental Psychology*, 10: 165–78.

Cohen, J. (1987) *Statistical Power Analysis for the Behavioral Sciences*, New York: Academic Press.

Colman, P. (1993) 'Psychological ageing', in J. Bond, P. Colman and S. M. Peace (eds) *Ageing in Society: An Introduction to Social Gerontology* (2nd edition), London: Sage.

Coleman, A. M. (1996) 'Teaching presentation skills to undergraduates: students' evaluation of a workshop course', *Psychology Teaching Review*, 5, 2: 75–82.

Conway, M. and Ross, M. (1984) 'Getting what you want by revising what you had', *Journal of Personality and Social Psychology*, 47, 4: 738–48.

Creanor, L., Durndell, H. and Primrose, C. (1996) 'Library and study skills using hypertext: the TILT experience', *The New Review of Hypermedia and Multimedia*, 2, 121–47.

Cuthbert, K. (1995) ' An innovative approach to teaching undergraduate psychology: rationale for a major final year project and some evaluative evidence', *Psychology Teaching Review*, 4, 1: 52–64.

Dale, R. and Douglas, S. (1996) 'Two investigations into intelligent text processing', in M. Sharples and T. van der Geest (eds) *The New Writing Environment: Writers at Work in a World of Technology*, London: Springer.

Daniel, J. (1996) *Mega-universities and Knowledge Media*, London: Kogan Page.

Davidson, M. J. (1996) 'Women and employment', in P. B. Warr (ed.) *Psychology at Work* (4th edition), London: Penguin Books.

Davies, B. and Harré, R. (1989) 'Introduction to special issue: gender, education and current issues', *Oxford Review of Education*, 15, 3: 213–14.

Dennis, I. and Newstead, S. E. (1994) 'The strange case of the disappearing sex bias', *Assessment and Evaluation in Higher Education*, 15: 132–9.

Dennis, I., Newstead, S. E. and Wright, D. E. (1996) 'A new approach to exploring biases in educational assessment', *British Journal of Psychology*, 87, 4: 515–34.

Department for Education (1994) *Statistical Bulletin*, Issue No. 16/94, September.

Department for Education and Employment (DfEE) (1996) 'Lifetime learning: a policy framework', Sheffield: DfEE.

Diekhoff, G. M., La Bett, E. E., Clark, R. E., Williams, L. E., Francis, W. and Haines, V. J. (1996) 'College cheating: ten years later', *Research in Higher Education*, 37, 4: 487–502.

Domino, G. (1971) 'Interactive effects of achievement orientation and teaching style on academic achievement', *Journal of Educational Psychology*, 62: 427–431.

Driver, R., Squires, A., Rushworth, P. and Wood-Robinson, V. (1994) *Making Sense of Secondary Science: Research into Children's Ideas*, London: Routledge.

Duffy, T. M. and Jonassen, D. H. (eds) (1992) *Constructivism and the Technology of Instruction: A Conversation*, Hillsdale, NJ: Erlbaum.

Entwistle, N. J. and Brennan, T. (1971) 'The academic performance of students: 2. Types of successful students', *British Journal of Educational Psychology*, 41, 3: 268–76.

Entwistle, N. J. and Entwistle, A. C. (1991) 'Contrasting forms of understanding for degree examinations: the student experience and its implications', *Higher Education*, 22: 205–27.

Entwistle, N. J. and Ramsden, P. (1983) *Understanding Student Learning*, London: Croom Helm.

Ericsson, K. A. and Charness, N. (1994) 'Expert performance: its structure and acquisition', *American Psychologist*, 49, 8: 725–47.

Ertmer, P. A., Newby, T. J. and MacDougall, M. (1996) 'Students' responses and approaches to case-based instruction: the role of reflective self-regulation', *American Educational Research Journal*, 33, 3: 719–52.

Eysenck, H. J. (1995) *Genius: The Natural History of Creativity*, Cambridge: Cambridge University Press.

Eysenck, H. J. and Eysenck, M. W. (1985) *Personality and Individual Differences: A Natural Science Approach*, New York: Plenum.

Falchikov, N. (1995a) 'Peer feedback marking: developing peer assessment', *Innovations in Education and Training International*, 32, 2: 176–87.

Falchikov, N. (1995b) 'Improving feedback to and from students', in P. Knight (ed.) *Assessment for Learning in Higher Education*, London: Kogan Page.

Fazey, D. M. A. (1993) 'Self-assessment as a generic skill for enterprising students: the learning process', *Assessment and Evaluation in Higher Education*, 18, 3: 235–50.

Fazey, D. M. A. and Linford, J. G. (1996) 'Tutoring for autonomous learning: principles and practice', *Innovations in Education and Training International*, 33, 3: 185–96.

Feitler, F. C. *et al.* (1971) Study reported in *Psychology Today*, September, p. 12.

Finlay, I., Maughan, T. S. and Webster, D. J. T. (1994) 'Portfolio learning: a proposal for undergraduate cancer teaching', *Medical Education*, 28, 1: 79–82.

Flora, S. R. and Logan, R. E. (1996) 'Using computerized study guides to increase performance on general psychology examinations: an experimental analysis', *Psychological Reports*, 19: 234–41.

Fox, J. A. (1989) 'Dynamic rules for user interface design'. Paper available from the author, Mitre Corporation, Bedford, MA 01730, USA.

Freeman, M. (1995) 'Peer assessment by groups of group work', *Assessment and Evaluation in Higher Education*, 20, 3: 289–300.

Fryer, M. (1996) *Creative Teaching and Learning*, London: Paul Chapman.

Garvin, J. W., Butcher, A. C., Stefani, L. A. J., Tariq, V. N., Lewis, M. H. R., Blumson, N. L., Govier, R. N. and Hill, J. A. (1995) 'Group projects for first-year university students: an evaluation', *Assessment and Evaluation in Higher Education*, 20, 3: 273–88.

Getzels, J. W. and Jackson, P. W. (1962) *Creativity and Intelligence: Explorations with Gifted Students*, New York: Wiley.

Gibbs, G. (ed.) (1992) *Improving the Quality of Student Learning*, Bristol: Technical and Educational Services Ltd.

Gibbs, G. (ed.) (1994) *Improving Student Learning: Theory and Practice*, Oxford: Oxford Centre for Staff Development, Oxford Brookes University.

Gibbs, G. (ed.) (1995) *Improving Student Learning through Assessment and Evaluation*, Oxford: Oxford Centre for Staff Development, Oxford Brookes University.

Gibbs, G. (ed.) (1996) *Improving Student Learning: Using Research to Improve Student Learning*, Oxford: Oxford Centre for Staff Development, Oxford Brookes University.

Gibbs, G., Lucas, L. and Simonite, V. (1996) 'Class size and student performance: 1984–94', *Studies in Higher Education*, 21, 3: 261–74.

Gibbs, G., Morgan, A. R. and Taylor, E. (1997) 'The world of the learner', in F. Marton, D. Hounsell and N. Entwistle (eds) *The Experience of Learning* (2nd edition), Edinburgh: Scottish Academic Press.

Gill, J. (1996) *Telecommunications: The Missing Links for People with Disabilities*, London: Royal National Institute for the Blind.

Girden, E. R. (1996) *Evaluating Research Articles from Start to Finish*, London: Sage.

Goldman, B. A. and Flake, W. L. (1996) 'Is flexibility related to college achievement? A five-year study', *Psychological Reports*, 78: 337–8.

Grammatik 5 (1992) Reference Software International: 25 Bourne Court, Southen Road, Woodford Green, Essex IG8 8HD, UK.

Greenwood, K. M. (1995) 'An evaluation of the Circadian Type Questionnaire', *Ergonomics*, 38, 2: 347–60.

Griffin, C. C. and Tulbert, B. L. (1995) 'The effect of graphic organisers on students' comprehension and recall of expository text: a review of the research and implications for practice', *Reading and Writing Quarterly: Overcoming Learning Difficulties* 11: 73–89.

Grundy, F. (1996) *Women and Computers*, Oxford: Intellect.

Haas, C. (1996) *Writing Technology: Studies on the Materiality of Literacy*, Mahwah, NJ: Erlbaum.

Hall, H. and McMurdo, G. (1993) 'Hand written or word processed? The option of submitting word processed exam scripts', paper available from the authors, Department of Communication and Information Studies, Queen Margaret College, Edinburgh EH12 8TS.

Halpern, D. E. (1992) *Sex Differences in Cognitive Abilities* (2nd edition), Hillsdale, NJ: Erlbaum.

Halpern, D. E. (1996) *Thought and Knowledge: An Introduction to Critical Thinking* (3rd edition), Mahwah, NJ: Erlbaum.

Hampson, L. (1994) *How's Your Dissertation Going?* Lancaster: Lancaster University School of Independent Studies.

Hansen, N. E. and Gladfelter, J. (1996) 'Teaching graduate psychology seminars using electronic mail: creative distance education', *Teaching of Psychology*, 23, 4: 252–6.

Harris, I. (1995) 'Learning contracts – related assessment issues', in P. Knight (ed.) *Assessment for Learning in Higher Education*, London: Kogan Page.

Harris, R. (1996) 'Variation among style checkers in sentence measurement', *TEXT Technology*, 6, 2: 80–90.

Hartley, A. and Paris, C. (1997) 'Multilingual document production: from support for translating to support for authoring', *Machine Translation*, 12, 1–2: 109–29.

Hartley, J. (1983) 'Notetaking research: re-setting the scoreboard', *Bulletin of the British Psychological Society*, 36: 13–14.

Hartley, J. (1984) 'The role of colleagues and text-editing programs in improving text', *IEEE Transactions on Professional Communication* P–C 27, 1: 42–4.

Hartley, J. (1994) *Designing Instructional Text* (3rd edition), London: Kogan Page.

Hartley, J. and Branthwaite, A. J. (1977) 'Course-work assessment: computer-aided decision making', in P. Hills and J. Gilbert (eds) *Aspects of Educational Technology 11*, London: Kogan Page.

Hartley, J. and Greggs, M. A. (1997) 'Divergent thinking in arts and science students: *Contrary Imaginations* at Keele revisited', *Studies in Higher Education*, 22, 1: 93–7.

Hartley, J. and Trueman, M. (1997) 'What's the bottom line? How well do mature students do at university?', in P. Sutherland (ed.) *Adult Learning: A Reader*, London: Kogan Page.

Hartley, J., Trueman, M. and Lapping, C. (1997) 'The academic performance of mature and traditional entry students: a review and a case-study', *Journal of Access Studies*, 12, 1: 98–112.

Hartog, P. and Rhodes, E. C. (1936) *The Marks of Examiners*, London: Macmillan.

Hastings, N., Schweiso, J. and Wheldhall, K. (1996) 'A place for learning', in P. Croll and N. Hastings (eds) *Effective Primary Teaching*, London: David Fulton.

Hawkridge, D. and Vincent, T. (1994) *Learning Difficulties and Computers: Access to the Curriculum*, London: Jessica Kingsley.

Hay, I. and Miller, R. (1992). 'Application of a poster exercise in an advanced undergraduate geography course', *Journal of Geography in Higher Education*, 16, 2: 199–215.

Hayes, J. and Allinson, C. (1996) 'The implications of learning styles for training and development: a discussion of the matching hypothesis', *British Journal of Management*, 7: 63–73.

Hayes, K. and Richardson, J. T. E. (1995) 'Gender, subject and context as determinants of approaches to studying in higher education', *Studies in Higher Education*, 20, 2: 215–21.

Heffernan, T. M. (1997) *A Student's Guide to Studying Psychology*, Hove: Psychology Press.

Hegarty, J. (ed.) (1991) *Into the 1990s: The Present and Future of Microcomputers for People with Learning Difficulties*, Stoke-on-Trent: Change Publications.

Henry, J. (1994) *Teaching Through Projects*, London: Kogan Page.

Hess, T. M. (1994) 'Social cognition in adulthood: aging-related changes in knowledge and processing mechanisms', *Developmental Review*, 14: 373–412.

Hettich, P. (1976) 'The journal: an autobiographical approach to learning', *Teaching of Psychology*, 3, 2: 60–1.

Hettich, P. (1990) 'Journal writing: old fare or nouvelle cuisine?', *Teaching of Psychology*, 17, 1: 36–9.

Hettich, P. (1992) *Learning Skills for College and Career*, Pacific Grove, CA: Brooks Cole.

Hilgard, E. R. and Bower, G. H. (1975) *Theories of Learning* (4th edition), Englewood Cliffs, NJ: Prentice-Hall.

Hofer, B. K. and Pintrich, P. R. (1997) 'The development of epistemological theories: beliefs about knowing and their relation to learning', *Review of Educational Research*, 67, 1: 88–140.

Holt, J. (1982a) *How Children Learn*, Harmondsworth: Penguin.

Holt, J. (1982b) *How Children Fail*, Harmondsworth: Penguin.

Hounsell, D. (1997) 'Contrasting conceptions of essay writing', in F. Marton, D. Hounsell and N. Entwistle (eds) *The Experience of Learning* (2nd edition), Edinburgh: Scottish Academic Press.

Houston, K. and Lazenbatt, A. (1996) 'The introduction and evaluation of peer-tutoring in undergraduate courses', *Journal of Further and Higher Education*, 20, 1: 39–50.

Howarth, I. and Croudace, T. (1995) 'Improving the quality of teaching in universities: a problem for occupational psychologists?', *Psychology Teaching Review*, 4, 1: 1–39.

Howells, K. and Piggott, S. (1992) 'Guided reading in biology: a modified Keller system', in G. Gibbs and A. Jenkins (eds) *Teaching Large Classes in Higher Education*, London: Kogan Page.

Hudson, L. (1966) *Contrary Imaginations*, London: Methuen.

Jonassen, D. H. (1989) *Hypertext/Hypermedia*, Englewood Cliffs, NJ: Educational Technology Publications.

Jonassen, D. H. and Grabowski, B. L. (1993) *Handbook of Individual Differences, Learning, and Instruction*, Hillsdale, NJ: Erlbaum.

Jordan, S. and Yeomans, D. (1991) 'Wither independent learning? The politics of curricular and pedagogical change in a polytechnic department', *Studies in Higher Education*, 16, 3: 291–308.

REFERENCES

Kaldeway, J. and Korthagen, F. A. J. (1995) 'Training in studying in higher education: objectives and effects', *Higher Education*, 30: 81–95.

Kazdin, A. E. (1994) *Behavior Modification in Applied Settings*, New York: Brooks Cole.

Keller, F. (1968) '"Goodbye teacher . . ."', *Journal of Applied Behavioral Analysis*, 1: 79–89.

Kellogg, R. T. (1994) *The Psychology of Writing*, New York: Oxford University Press.

Kelly, A. E. and O'Donnell, A. (1994) 'Hypertext and study strategies of preservice teachers: issues in instructional hypertext design', *Journal of Educational Computing Research*, 10, 4: 373–87.

King, A. (1992) 'A comparison of self-questioning, summarising and note-taking review as strategies for learning from lectures', *American Educational Research Journal*, 29, 2: 303–24.

King, E. (1994) 'An investigation into the learning experiences of mature students entering higher education', in G. Gibbs (ed.) *Improving Student Learning: Theory and Practice*, Oxford: Oxford Centre for Staff Development, Oxford Brookes University.

Kirby, J. R. (1993). 'Collaborative and competitive effects of verbal and spatial processes', *Learning and Instruction*, 3: 201–14.

Kirkman, J. (1994) *Guidelines for Giving Effective Presentations*, Marlborough: Ramsbury Books.

Knapper, C. K. (1988) 'Technology and life-long learning', in D. Boud (ed.) (1988) *Developing Student Autonomy* (2nd edition), London: Kogan Page.

Knapper, C. K. (1995) 'Approaches to study and lifelong learning: some Canadian initiatives', in G. Gibbs (ed.) *Improving Student Learning Through Assessment and Evaluation*, Oxford: Oxford Centre for Staff Development, Oxford Brookes University.

Kniveton, B. (1996) 'Student perceptions of assessment methods', *Assessment and Evaluation in Higher Education*, 21, 3: 229–37.

Knowles, M. S. (1986) *Using Learning Contracts*, San Francisco: Jossey Bass.

Kohut, G. F. and Gorman, K. J. (1995) 'The effectiveness of leading grammar/style software packages in analyzing business students' writing', *Journal of Business and Technical Communication*, 9, 3: 341–61.

Kosnik, W., Winslow, L., Kline, D., Rasinski, K. and Sekuler, R. (1988) 'Visual changes in daily life throughout adulthood', *Journal of Gerontology: Psychological Sciences*, 43, 3: 63–70.

Kulik, J. A., Kulik, C.-L. C. and Cohen, P. A. (1979) 'A meta-analysis of outcome studies of Keller's personalised system of instruction', *American Psychologist*, 34, 4: 307–18.

Kulik, J. A., Kulik, C.-L. C. and Cohen, P. A. (1980) 'Effectiveness of computer-based college teaching: a meta-analysis of findings', *Review of Educational Research*, 50, 4: 525–44.

Kwok, M. and Jones, C. (1995) 'Catering for different learning styles', *ALT Journal*, 3, 1: 5–11.

Landauer, T., Egan, D., Remde, J., Lesk, M., Lochbaum, C. and Ketchum, D. (1993) 'Enhancing the usability of text through computer delivery and formative evaluation: the SuperBook project', in C. McKnight, A. Dillon and J. Richardson (eds) *Hypertext: A Psychological Perspective*, Hemel Hempstead: Ellis Horwood.

Laurillard, D. (1979). 'The process of student learning', *Higher Education*, 8, 4: 395–410.

Leopold, J. W. and Osborne, M. (1996) 'The performance of former in-house Access students at a Scottish University', *Journal of Access Studies*, 11, 1: 120–31.

Lipsey, M. W. and Wilson, D. B. (1993) 'The efficacy of psychological, educational, and behavioral treatment: confirmation from meta-analysis', *American Psychologist*, 48, 12: 1181–209.

Lister, I. (ed.) (1974) *De-schooling: A Reader*, Cambridge: Cambridge University Press.

Liu, M. and Reed, W. M. (1994) 'The relationship between the learning strategies and learning styles in a hypermedia environment', *Computers in Human Behavior*, 10, 4: 419–34.

Maccoby, E. E. and Jacklin, C. N. (1974) *The Psychology of Sex Differences*, London: Oxford University Press.

McCrindle, A. R. and Christensen, C. A. (1995) 'The impact of learning journals on metacognitive processes and learning performance', *Learning and Instruction*, 5, 3: 167–85.

McDowell, L. (1993) 'Enterprise education and part-time students', *Assessment and Evaluation in Higher Education*, 18, 3: 187–203.

McGilly, K. (ed.) (1994) *Classroom Lessons: Integrating Cognitive Theory and Classroom Practice*, Cambridge, MA: MIT Press.

McGlade, K., Toal, C. and Kernohan, G. (1996) 'An electronic learning diary', *Active Learning*, 4: 42–5.

McKeachie, W. J. (1994) *Teaching Tips: Strategies, Research, and Theory for College and University Teachers* (9th edition), Lexington, MA: Heath.

McKnight, C., Dillon, A. and Richardson, J. (eds) (1993) *Hypertext: A Psychological Perspective*, Hemel Hempstead: Ellis Horwood.

McNamara, D. and Harris, R. (eds) (1997) *Overseas Students in Higher Education: Issues in Teaching and Learning*, London: Routledge.

Mahalaski, P. A. (1992) 'Essay-writing: do study manuals give relevant advice?', *Higher Education*, 24: 113–32.

Marshall, J. G. and Powers, J. M. (1969) Writing neatness, composition errors and essay grades', *Journal of Educational Measurement*, 6, 2: 97–101.

Marton, F. and Saljo, R. (1976) 'On qualitative differences in student learning: 1. Outcome and process', *British Journal of Educational Psychology*, 46, 1: 4–11.

Menges, R. (1994) 'Teaching in the age of electronic information', in W. J. McKeachie *Teaching Tips: Strategies, Research, and Theory for College and University Teachers* (9th edition), Lexington, MA: Heath.

Millar, R. and Irving, P. (1995) 'Academic locus of control in British undergraduate students', *British Journal of Educational Psychology*, 65, 3: 331–40.

Mooney, G. A., Bligh, J. G., Leinster, L. and Warenius, H. M. (1995) 'An electronic study guide for problem-based learning', *Medical Education*, 29: 397–402.

Moreland, R., Miller, J. and Laucka, F. (1981) 'Academic achievement and self-evaluation of academic performance', *Journal of Educational Psychology*, 73, 3: 335–44.

Morgan, A. (1993) *Improving Your Students' Learning: Reflections on the Experience of Study*, London: Kogan Page.

National Union of Students (1996) 'Students at work: a report on the economic conditions of students in employment', London: National Union of Students.

Neufeld, V. and Barrows, H. S. (1974) 'The "McMaster Philosophy": an approach to medical education', *Journal of Medical Education*, 49, 11: 1040–50.

Newstead, S. E. (1992) 'A study of two "quick-and-easy" methods of assessing individual differences in student learning', *British Journal of Educational Psychology*, 62, 3: 299–312.

Newstead, S. E. (1996) 'The psychology of student assessment', *The Psychologist*, 9, 12: 543–7.

Newstead, S. E., Franklyn-Stokes, A. and Armstead, P. (1996) 'Individual differences in student cheating', *Journal of Educational Psychology*, 88, 2: 229–41.

Nicholson, N. (1977) 'Counselling the adult learner in the Open University', *Teaching at a Distance*, 8: 62–9.

Nisbet, J. and Welsh, J. (1972) 'The mature student', *Educational Research*, 14, 3: 204–7.

Norton, L. S. (1990) 'Essay writing: what really counts?', *Higher Education*, 20: 411–42.

Norton, L. S. and Crowley, C. M. (1995) 'Can students be helped to learn how to learn? An evaluation of an Approaches to Learning programme for first year degree students', *Higher Education*, 29: 307–28.

Norton, L. S. and Dickins, T. E. (1995) 'Do Approaches to Learning Courses improve students' learning strategies?', in G. Gibbs (ed.) *Improving Student Learning through Assessment and Evaluation*, Oxford: Oxford Centre for Staff Development, Oxford Brookes University.

Norton, L. S. and Hartley, J. (1986) 'What factors contribute to good examination marks? The role of notetaking in subsequent examination performance', *Higher Education*, 15: 355–71.

Norton, L., Dickins, T. and McGlaughlin Cook, N. (1996) 'Coursework assessment: what are tutors really looking for?', in G. Gibbs (ed.) *Improving Student Learning: Using Research to Improve Student Learning*, Oxford: Oxford Centre for Staff Development, Oxford Brookes University.

Nulty, D. D. and Barrett, M. A. (1996) 'Transitions in students' learning styles', *Studies in Higher Education*, 21, 3: 333–45.

Nye, P. A., Crooks, T. J., Powley, M. and Tripp, G. (1984) 'Student note-taking related to university examination performance', *Higher Education*, 13: 85–97.

O'Connell, C., Arnold, P. and Meudell, P. (1995) 'Evaluation of the practical tutorial', *Psychology Teaching Review*, 4, 1: 68–71.

O'Donnell, A. and Dansereau, D. F. (1994) 'Learning from lectures: effects of cooperative review', *Journal of Experimental Education*, 61, 2: 116–25.

Oliver, R. and Kerr, T. (1993) 'The impact of word processing on the preparation and submission of written essays in a tertiary course of study', *Higher Education*, 26, 2: 217–26.

Paice, C. (1994) 'Automatic abstracting', in A. Kent (ed.) *Encyclopaedia of Library and Information Science* (Vol. 3, Supplement 16), pp. 16–27, New York: Dekker Inc.

Papert, S. (1993) *The Children's Machine: Rethinking School in the Age of the Computer*, Hemel Hempstead: Harvester Wheatsheaf.

Pascall, G. and Cox, R. (1993) *Women Returning to Higher Education*, Milton Keynes: Open University Press.

Paterson, P. and Rosbottom, J. (1995) 'Learning style and learning strategies in a multimedia environment', *ALT Journal*, 3, 1: 12–21.

Pear, J. J. and Novak, M. (1996) 'Computer-aided personalized system of instruction: a program evaluation', *Teaching of Psychology*, 23, 2: 119–123.

Peck, K. L. and Hannafin, M. J. (1983) 'The effects of notetaking pretraining and the recording of notes on the retention of aural instruction', *Journal of Educational Research*, 77, 2: 100–7.

Pennington, M. C. (1993) 'Computer-assisted writing on a principled basis: the case against computer-assisted text analysis for non-proficient writers', *Language and Education*, 7, 1: 43–59.

Percy, K. and Ramsden, P. (1980) *Independent Study: Two examples from English Higher Education*, Guildford, Surrey: Society for Research into Higher Education.

Perera, D. and Hartley, J. (1997) 'The costs of crowded classrooms', *New Academic*, 6, 2: 17–18.

Perry, W. G. (1970) *Forms of Intellectual and Ethical Development in the College Years: A Scheme*, New York: Holt, Rinehart & Winston.

Pirkl, J. (1994) *Transgenerational Design: Products for an Aging Population*, New York: Van Nostrand Reinhold.

Portier, S. J. and van Buuren, H. A. (1995) 'An interactive learning environment (ILE) to study statistics: effects of prior knowledge on the use of embedded support devices', *European Journal of Psychology of Education*, X, 2: 197–207.

Potterton, V. A. and Parsons, P. G. (1995) 'Qualitative changes in learning and teaching brought about by using records of student achievement', in G. Gibbs (ed.) *Improving Student Learning Through Assessment and Evaluation*, Oxford: Oxford Centre for Staff Development, Oxford Brookes University.

Pratt, D. D. (1992) 'Conceptions of teaching', *Adult Education Quarterly*, 42, 4: 203–20.

Prosser, M. and Webb, C. (1994) 'Relating the process of undergraduate essay writing to the finished product', *Studies in Higher Education*, 19, 2: 125–38.

Purdie, N. and Hattie, J. (1997) 'Cultural differences in the use of strategies for self-regulated learning', *American Educational Research Journal*, 33, 6: 845–71.

Radford, J. and Holdstock, L. (1995) 'Gender differences in higher education aims between Computing and Psychology students', *Research in Science and Technological Education*, 13, 2: 163–76.

Ramsden, P. (1992) *Learning to Teach in Higher Education*, London: Routledge.

Ramsden, P. and Entwistle, N. J. (1981) 'Effects of academic departments on students' approaches to studying', *British Journal of Educational Psychology*, 51: 368–83.

Reber, A. S. (1995) *The Penguin Dictionary of Psychology*, London: Penguin.

Reiser, R. A. (1987) ' Instructional technology: a history', in R. M. Gagné (ed.) *Educational Technology: Foundations*, Hillsdale, NJ: Erlbaum.

Richardson, J. T. E. (1997) 'Dispelling some myths about mature students in higher education: study skills, approaches to studying and intellectual ability', in P. Sutherland (ed.) *Adult Learning: A Reader*, London: Kogan Page.

Richardson, J. T. E. and King, E. (1997) 'Adult students in higher education', *Teaching of Psychology* (in press).

Rickards, T. (1992) *How to Win as a Mature Student*, London: Kogan Page.

Riding, R. J. and Rayner, S. G. (eds) (1997) 'Learning styles and strategies', *Educational Psychology*, 17, 1/2: 5–225.

Risko, V. J., Alvarez, M. C. and Fairbanks, M. (1991) 'Internal factors that influence study', in R. F. Flippo and D. C. Caverly (eds) *Teaching Reading and Study Strategies at the College Level*, Newark, DE: International Reading Association.

Robson, C. (1993) *Real World Research: A Resource for Social Scientists and Practioner-Researchers*, Oxford: Blackwell.

Roe, P. R. W. (ed.) (1995) *Telecommunications for All*, Luxembourg: Office for Official Publications of the European Communities.

Rogers, C. R. and Freiberg, H. J. (1994) *Freedom to Learn* (3rd edition), New York: Merrill.

Rosenberg, J. and Blount, R. L. (1988) 'Poster sessions revisited: a student research convocation', *Teaching of Psychology*, 15, 1: 38–9.

Rosenthal, R. and Jacobson, L. (1968) *Pygmalion in the Classroom*, New York: Holt, Rinehart & Winston.

Ross, L. L. and McBean, D. (1995) 'A comparison of pacing contingencies in classes using a personalized system of instruction', *Journal of Applied Behavior Analysis*, 28, 1: 87–8.

Rowntree, D. (1987) *Assessing Students: How Shall We Know Them?* (2nd edition), London: Kogan Page.

Rudd, E. (1984) 'A comparison between the results achieved by women and men studying for first degrees in British Education', *Studies in Higher Education*, 9, 1: 47–57.

Rudd, E. (1988) 'Reply to Clarke', *Studies in Higher Education*, 13, 3: 333–6.

Rust, C. and Gibbs, G. (eds) (1997) *Improving Student Learning: Improving Student Learning through Course Design*, Oxford: Oxford Centre for Staff Development, Oxford Brookes University.

Sadler-Smith, E. (1996) 'Approaches to studying: age, gender and academic performance', *Educational Studies*, 22, 3: 367–79.

Saettler, P. (1990). *The Evolution of American Educational Technology*, Englewood, CO: Libraries Unlimited.

Saljo, R. (1979) 'Learning about learning', *Higher Education*, 8: 443–51.

Santostefano, S. (1985) *Cognitive Control Therapy with Children and Adolescents*, New York: Pergamon.

Schank, R. C. and Cleary, C. (1995) *Engines for Education*, Hillsdale, NJ: Erlbaum.

Schunk, D. H. and Zimmerman, B. J. (eds) (1994) *Self-Regulation of Learning and Performance*, Hillsdale, NJ: Erlbaum.

Scott, J., Buchanan, J. and Haigh, N. (1997) 'Reflections on student-centred learning in a large class setting', *British Journal of Educational Technology*, 28, 1: 19–30.

Scouller, K. M. and Prosser, M. (1994) 'Students' experiences in studying for multiple choice question examinations', *Studies in Higher Education*, 19, 3: 267–79.

Sharples, M. (ed.) (1993) *Computer Supported Collaborative Writing*, London: Springer-Verlag.

Sharples, M. (1994) 'Computer support for the rhythms of writing', *Computers and Composition*, 11: 217–26.

Sharples, M. and van der Geest, T. (eds) (1996) *The New Writing Environment: Writers at Work in a World of Technology*, London: Springer.

Sharples, M., Goodlet, J. and Pemberton, L. (1989) 'Developing a writer's assistant', in N. Williams and P. Holt (eds) *Computers and Writing*, Oxford: Intellect Books.

Slotnick, H. B., Pelton, M. H., Fuller, M. L. and Tabor, L. (1993) *Adult Learners on Campus*, London: Taylor & Francis.

Smit, G. N. and van der Molen, H. T. (1996) 'Three methods for the assessment of communication skills', *British Journal of Educational Psychology*, 66, 4: 543–55.

Smith, B. and Brown, S. (eds) (1995) *Research, Teaching and Learning in Higher Education*, London: Kogan Page.

Smith, J. B. (1994) *Collective Intelligence in Computer-Based Collaboration*, Hillsdale, NJ: Erlbaum.

Smyth, T. R. (1996) *Writing in Psychology: A Student Guide* (2nd edition), New York: Wiley.

Stanton, H. (1988) 'Independent study: a matter of confidence', in D. Boud (ed.) *Developing Student Autonomy in Learning*, London: Kogan Page.

Starr, B. (1993) 'Profiling and assessment of professional and personal transferable skills acquired by students on a BSc honours course in psychology', in A. Assiter and E. Shaw (eds) *Using Records of Student Achievement in Higher Education*, London: Kogan Page.

Stephenson, J. (1988) 'The experience of Independent Studies at North East London Polytechnic', in D. Boud (ed.) *Developing Student Autonomy in Learning*, London: Kogan Page.

Stephenson, J. (1994) 'The student experience of independent study: reaching the parts other programmes appear to miss', in N. Graves (ed.) *Learner Managed Learning*, London: Kogan Page.

Sternberg, R. J. (1985) *Beyond IQ – A Triarchic Theory of Human Intelligence*, New York: Cambridge University Press.

Sternberg, R. J. (1995) *In Search of the Human Mind*, Fort Worth, TX: Harcourt Brace International.

Sutherland, P. (ed.) (1997) *Adult Learning: A Reader*, London: Kogan Page.

Swanson, D. B., Case, S. M. and van der Vleuten, C. P. M. (1997) 'Strategies for student assessment', in D. Boud and G. Feletti (eds) *The Challenge of Problem Based Learning*, London: Kogan Page.

Sydes, M. and Hartley, J. (1997) 'A thorn in the Flesch: observations on the unreliability of computer-based readability formulae', *British Journal of Educational Technology*, 28, 2: 143–5.

Tait, H., Speth, C. and Entwistle, N. (1995) 'Identifying and advising students with deficient study skills and strategies', in G. Gibbs (ed.) *Improving Student Learning Through Assessment and Evaluation*, Oxford: Oxford Centre for Staff Development, Oxford Brookes University.

Tennant, M. and Pogson, P. (1995) *Learning and Change in the Adult Years*, San Francisco: Jossey Bass.

Thacker, C. and Novak, M. (1991) 'Student role supports for younger and older middle-aged women: application of a life event model', *The Canadian Journal of Higher Education*, 21, 1: 13–36.

Thomas, K. (1988) 'Gender and the arts/science divide in higher education', *Studies in Higher Education*, 13, 2: 123–37.

Thompson, J. (1996) 'Embedding technology into language examinations: a case study', *Active Learning*, 4: 24–9.

Thyer, B. A. (1992) 'Walden "U": first report of a behaviorally based college', *Behavior and Social Issues*, 2, 2: 145–54.

Tobias, S. (1994) 'Interest, prior knowledge and learning', *Review of Educational Research*, 64, 1: 37–54.

Tomlinson, K. and Macfarlane, B. (1995) 'The significance of subject choice in explaining the first-class degree divide between male and female graduates', *Research in Education*, 54: 95–100.

Topping, K. J. (1996) 'The effectiveness of peer tutoring in further and higher education: a typology and a review of the literature', *Higher Education*, 32: 321–44.

Torrance, M., Thomas, G. V. and Robinson, E. J. (1994) 'The development of writing skills in social science undergraduates: expectations, experiences and strategies', poster paper presented at the EARLI/SIG Writing Conference, Utrecht, 19–21 October. (Available from the authors in the School of Psychology, Birmingham University, Birmingham B15 2TT.)

Torrance, M., Thomas, G. V. and Robinson, E. J. (1997) 'Strategies for academic writing: individual differences in the writing behavior of undergraduate students.' (Paper available from G. V. Thomas, School of Psychology, Birmingham University, Birmingham B15 2TT.)

Trueman, M. and Hartley, J. (1996) 'A comparison between the time-management skills and academic performance of mature and traditional-entry university students', *Higher Education*, 32: 199–215.

Van Meter, P., Yokoi, L. and Pressley, M. (1994) 'College students' theory of note-taking derived from their perceptions of note-taking', *Journal of Educational Psychology*, 86, 3: 323–38.

Velayo, R. S. and Venkateswaran, R. (1992) 'Using computer conferencing in teaching psychology: a case study', paper presented at the 100th Annual Convention of the American Psychological Association, Washington, DC. Copies available from Richard Velayo, 36061 Grand River Avenue, No. 102, Farmington, MI 48335, USA.

Vernon, D. T. A. and Blake, R. L. (1994) 'Does problem-based learning work? A meta-analysis of evaluative research', *Academic Medicine*, 69, 3: 550–63.

Wagner, R. and Sternberg, R. (1985) 'Practical intelligence in real-world pursuits: the role of tacit knowledge', *Journal of Personality and Social Psychology*, 49, 2: 436–55.

Wark, D. M. and Flippo, R. F. (1991) 'Preparing for and taking tests', in R. F. Flippo and D. C. Caverly (eds) *Teaching Reading and Study Strategies at the College Level*, Newark, DE: International Reading Association.

Warren, E. (1997) 'Sex bias in student assessments', unpublished MPhil thesis, University of Central Lancashire, Preston.

Watkins, D. A. and Hattie, J. (1981) 'The learning processes of Australian university students: investigations of contextual and personological factors', *British Journal of Educational Psychology*, 51: 384–93.

Wheldall, K. and Glynn, T. (1989) *Effective Classroom Learning*, Oxford: Blackwell.

Willcoxson, L. and Prosser, M. (1996) 'Kolb's Learning Style Inventory (1985): review and further study of validity and reliability', *British Journal of Educational Psychology*, 66, 2: 247–58.

Willis, S. L., Jay, G. M., Diehl, M. and Marsiske, M. (1992) 'Longitudinal change and prediction of everyday task competence in the elderly', *Research on Aging*, 14, 1: 68–91.

Winne, P. H., Gupta, L. and Nesbit, J. C. (1994) 'Exploring individual differences in studying strategies using graph theory statistics', *Alberta Journal of Educational Research*, 40, 2: 177–93.

Witkin, H. (1976) 'Cognitive style in academic performance and in teacher–student relations', in S. Messick and associates, *Individuality in Learning*, San Francisco, CA: Jossey Bass.

Wolfe, R. N. and Johnson, S. D. (1995) 'Personality as a predictor of college performance', *Educational and Psychological Measurement*, 55, 2: 177–85.

Wong, C. T., Day, J. J., Maxwell, S. E. and Meara, N. M. (1995) 'A multitrait-multimethod study of academic and social intelligence in college students', *Journal of Educational Psychology*, 87, 1: 117–33.

Yule, W. and Carr, J. (eds) (1987) *Behaviour Modification for People with Mental Handicaps* (2nd edition), London: Chapman & Hall.

Zeidner, M. (1996) ' How do high school and college students cope with test situations', *British Journal of Educational Psychology*, 66, 1: 115–28.

Zwahr, M. (1998) 'Cognitive processes utilized in making decisions about medical treatment', in D. C. Park, R. W. Morrell and K. Shifren (eds) *Processing of Medical Information in Aging Patients: Cognitive and Human Factors Perspectives*, Mahwah, NJ: Erlbaum (in press).

Index